On Writing Fiction

Third Edition

Some editors are failed writers, but so are most writers.

—T. S. Eliot

On Writing Fiction

Third Edition

Quinn Tyler Jackson

Unattributed short story and poem excerpts in this book are from stories and poems by the author that have appeared in *The Ampersand*, *Apotheosis: Journal of the Poetic Genius Society*, *Distant Worlds*, *Drop the Buddha*, *The Kudzu Monthly*, *Lost Cause Quarterly*, *Noesis-E*, *Tickled by Thunder*, and *Ubiquity: Journal of the Ultranet*.

Unattributed novel excerpts are from the author's novels published by PlaneTree Press, UK, and Chevalier Editions. The PlaneTree Press editions are now out of print, but are available from Chevalier Editions.

Excerpts from other authors are noted in the text as to author and title.

Epigrams quoting the poet Fred Candelaria are from the author's "Interview with Fred Candelaria, West Coast Poet," *Tickled by Thunder*, Vol. 5 No. 14, 1994. Other epigrams are from various sources.

This book was developed in part from *On Writing the Short Story: A Mad Tea Party*, published in 2003 by Tickled by Thunder Press.

Authors, readers, and generic characters, when mentioned in the singular herein, are referred to in the masculine singular forms. Either gender may be assumed except where context dictates it is ridiculous to do so.

Table of Contents

Introduction

I can just see a new generation of writers laboriously 'teaching' their settings, cutting the heads and tails off their scenes, and making up single sentences to describe entire novels instead of just writing the damn things. Geez Louise, if we could say it in one sentence we'd stop there, it'd be easier.

—Pamela C. Dean

This book is not a compilation of *rules* that will somehow turn a lumberjack, grocery clerk, dentist, lawyer, or brain surgeon into an author of serious fiction. It is my hope, however, that lumberjacks, grocery clerks, dentists, lawyers, or brain surgeons wishing to expand their understanding of writing fiction will get something useful out of what will be presented. Even so, they will not get a list of *Dos and Don'ts* about writing; fiction writing does not at all answer to such lists. This book is also not at all about how to get published.

Instead, this book will examine in some detail the art of writing tight, coherent, meaningful fiction. New ideas offered, old ideas reexamined, and suggestions for artistic growth, but no hard and fast formulas or rules will be offered.

A DEFINITION OF "SERIOUS" FICTION

Although this book is about writing "serious" and "meaningful" fiction, I hesitate to say that it is about writing "literary" fiction. Genre fiction can be serious and meaningful, or it can be formulaic. Mainstream fiction, the same.

Whether a story takes place on Moon or Mars, one hundred years in the past or future, or on an alternative earth populated by dragons is not a marker of its meaningfulness or meaninglessness. I define serious and meaningful fiction as fiction that attempts to offer the reader some insight into the human condition.

This book, then, is probably not for the writer of escapist fiction that has as its goal simply to entertain or amuse, but wishes to push no boundary beyond that. There *is* a respectable place for such fiction. In fact, in many cases, such fiction can be just as difficult (or more!) to write as the so-called serious variety. Such fiction, however, shall not be discussed herein.

THE STRUCTURE OF THIS BOOK

The structure of this book is based in large part on the structure of my earlier booklet, *On Writing the Short Story*, with some additions and exclusions. The earlier booklet, due to length constraints and the narrowness of the form discussed, did not venture into some of these topics. The booklet ended with exercises for authors; the present work does not.

First, in addressing the mechanics of writing fiction, subjects such as forms of fiction, points of view, the passage of time, and dialog (amongst other topics) will be addressed. These notions have been categorized as *mechanical* because they are, in my view, less about beauty and art than they are about the nuts and bolts of fiction.

Second, some thoughts on aesthetic issues will be presented. These topics are necessarily more subjective than the pure nuts and bolts, even though some of the mechanical issues are, too, somewhat subjective. In this second section, I will offer far less concrete observations and advice, and instead speak in a more abstract tone.

The third and final section of this book discusses issues that are neither so much about mechanics nor so much about aesthetics as they are about *authors* themselves. This section, although adapted in part from essays on failure and growth, is totally new to the second and subsequent editions as it appears herein, and was not at all covered in *On Writing the Short Story*. Ego, honesty, artistic growth, and some of the possible pitfalls and joys of the artistic life of the author of fiction. This section, even more than the first two sections, will venture into personal opinion and observations. Those who don't care for such ruminations had best skip Part 3.

Authors, readers, and generic characters, when mentioned in the singular herein, are referred to in the masculine singular forms. Either gender may be assumed except where context dictates it is ridiculous to do so.

A WORD ON THE EXCERPTS

What a good thing Adam had. When he said a good thing he knew nobody had said it before.

—Mark Twain

Before continuing, please let me explain why I have primarily used my own fiction as examples in this book. In electing to point to my own work by way of example, I am at risk of appearing self-important. Well, by writing a book on writing fiction, I'm already at great risk of that, but please bear with me a moment while I apologize.

I have not chosen my own work for the examples because I'm particularly fond of seeing myself in print and want to pat myself on the back. I have two reasons: first, since I own the copyright on these works, I can cite them freely (and mutilate them for effect if necessary) without having to hunt down permission and payees; second, since I wrote them, I am uniquely qualified to comment on my *intent*. Whether or not my intent and the actual effect achieved are congruous, I shall let you decide. This book is, after all, about the *writing of,* rather than merely the *reading of,* fiction. I may be able to read Hemingway's *The Old Man and the Sea* and analyze what I see, or even read analyses of the story done by others, and comment as a bystander on some of what has been achieved, but I can never comment on Hemingway's *intent,* or whether or not he considers that the devices he used did those intentions justice. Since this is a book about writing fiction, to comment at that level about another's work would be, in my opinion, greater hubris than simply resorting to using as examples fiction I have myself written.

There will be, however, some exceptions, and these drawn from classics that have passed into the public domain. That I have placed my own work alongside such classics is an accident of selection more than comparison; the public domain works cited are simply the most readily available for such inclusion, and amongst those I have analyzed in sufficient depth to so include. In these cases, the discussion shall not be about *intent* but about the perceived *overall effect,* or to illustrate a point, if that excerpt does, indeed, seem to make the point more clear. London, Hamsun, Austen, and Maugham may well have chosen to disagree.

Part 1: Mechanics

"If you don't mind stopping the boat for a minute."

"How am *I* to stop it?' said the Sheep. "If you leave off rowing, it'll stop of itself."

So the boat was left to drift down the stream as it would, till it glided gently in among the waving rushes. And then the little sleeves were carefully rolled up, and the little arms were plunged in elbow-deep, to get hold of the rushes a good long way down before breaking them off—and for a while Alice forgot all about the Sheep and the knitting, as she bent over the side of the boat, with just the ends of her tangled hair dipping into the water—while with bright eager eyes she caught at one bunch after another of the darling scented rushes.

"I only hope the boat wo'n't tipple over!" she said to herself.

—Lewis Carroll, *Through the Looking-Glass*

In this section on mechanics I am not going to discuss manuscript margin widths or font selections, but rather, the rowing of the fictional boat. The reader who does not yet know how to get words onto a page in an acceptable format is expected to find that information somewhere else.

Forms of Fiction

Truth is shorter than fiction.

—Irving Cohen

Fiction comes in various forms, the three forms that shall be briefly discussed here being the short story, novella, and novel.

SHORT STORIES

We need only here say, upon this topic, that, in almost all classes of composition, the unity of effect or impression is a point of the greatest importance. It is clear, moreover, that this unity cannot be thoroughly preserved in productions whose perusal cannot be completed at one sitting.

—Edgar Allan Poe, in his criticism of Hawthorne's *Twice Told Tales*

Less than a novella, more cohesive than a chapter of a novel, but sometimes able to serve as one ... the short story is a curious literary beast. The well-executed short story is not merely a novella that never quite found its sea legs; it has its own *raison-d'être*. It does not apologize for being short; it stands alone, ultimately readable "at one sitting." Since various readers read fiction at different rates, the notion of "one sitting" is, in fact, not entirely an accurate metric. My daughters can (and often do) read entire novels at one sitting, as I once did. One might do well to remember that, in Poe's time, novels tended to be extremely long, perhaps tediously so by today's standards, and thus were nearly impossible to read in one sitting. Whether or not a vignette, that is, a short, descriptive literary "sketch" is, in fact, a form of short story is a pedagogic matter, and herein the terms are both encompassed in the use of the term short story.

NOVELLAS

[The novella] is one of the richest and most rewarding of literary forms ... it allows for more extended development of theme and character than does the short story, without making the elaborate structural demands of the full-length book. Thus it provides an intense, detailed exploration of its subject, providing to some degree both the concentrated focus of the short story and the broad scope of the novel.

—Robert Silverberg, *Sailing to Byzantium*

Longer than a short story, but not quite a novel, the novella is a stranger beast than the short story.

I urge you to avoid considering the novella to be simply a novel that ran out of steam, or a short story that got too big for its britches, since the novella, in its fullest form, is a literary form unto itself. Which elements are most explored in a novella is a decision that must be made if the piece is to flow well. Whether one elects to develop theme, character, the plot line, or even setting, is a matter that answers to the work, but a matter that must be resolved.

If not, novellas can read as if they are short stories that perhaps ought to have given up at some point and admitted their limited scope, or as novels that remained underdeveloped.

It might be entirely possible, then, to remove half (or more) of a full novel, and not end up with a novella, if what remains suggests, promises, or opens avenues that are never adequately explored. That is, length is not the only criterion as to what makes a novella neither a short story nor a novel.

NOVELS

The only obligation to which in advance we may hold a novel, without incurring the accusation of being arbitrary, is that it be interesting.

—Henry James

Novels, because of their length, afford the author the opportunity to address matters deeply, broadly, or both, in ways not available through the short story or novella. Plots may be more intricately woven, characters more carefully developed, and themes more comprehensively explored than in the shorter forms.

A danger of novels, however, is that they may contain too many words.* By this I do not mean the sheer length of the thing, but rather, the notion that some authors seem to espouse that because novels are longer than novellas and short stories, they should pad them with words just to make them *long*. Believe it or not, authors have been asked by publishers to pad out shorter works by some specific amount to make them longer. Every word in a well-executed novel *should* be there, should have just as much purpose as every word of a shorter form. That purpose might differ from the purpose of a word in a shorter form, but that purpose should exist. ♦

Regardless of its length, a novel, as I understand it to be, is a sustained fictional work that is unified in space or time, or both. This unification is what makes *Abadoun* a novel, even though it might be read also as a collection of short stories. Each chapter, although told from the point of view of a different character, is unified with each other by place (space), in that the stories all occur in or near the

---

* The probably apocryphal comment from Emperor Joseph II on Mozart's first Viennese opera *Die Entführung aus dem Serail* being: "Too many notes, my dear Mozart, and too beautiful for our ears."

♦ It is this adherence to purpose of every word that makes a work "too beautiful," for the Emperor's ears, and is Mozart's saving grace, after all.

town of Abadoun, and in time, since they all relate to the last day of the life of the village people so discussed. As already mentioned, even though I consider *Abadoun* to be a novel proper, it has been called a novella by reviewers because of its actual word count.

Points of View

"Suppose we change the subject," the March Hare interrupted, yawning. "I'm getting tired of this. I vote the young lady tells us a story."

"I'm afraid I don't know one," said Alice, rather alarmed at the proposal.

"Then the Dormouse shall!" they both cried.

—Lewis Carroll, *Alice in Wonderland*

The decision of which character's point of view (POV) from which to tell a story is an important one that effects the outcome of the entire work. After all, the reader will see everything from the eyes, hear everything from the ears, and feel everything through the senses of the POV character, and the writer must sustain that viewpoint throughout the narrative if the short piece is to be consistent and cohesive.

Selecting an appropriate narrative POV is not only important because of *how* things are told, but what *can* be told. If it is your desire as an author to speak of the inner feelings of more than one character in the story, for instance, you are pretty much forbidden (unless you wish to take risks) from using the first or second person POV. Selecting a POV, then, is a decision that comes after much consideration.

FIRST PERSON

Some writers and readers like the first person for the immediate sense of intimacy it can create. When a story is told as if the narrator were personally involved in the goings-on, using such words as *I* and *we,* a certain degree of directness is established. Readers can come to identify with such narrators quickly, if the timing and mood is right, and much work can sometimes be avoided in setting up the protagonist's character through his actions, since the reader gets an insider's view.

One of the primary dangers of the first person POV is that it can alienate some readers if the narrator is someone with whom they cannot easily form an empathetic bond. A self-indulgent and antisocial character who enjoys torturing small animals, for instance, may be more easy to digest from the distance of the impersonal third person *he* than the first person *I,* since many readers will not share this deviant joy in torture. A first person narrator need not even be particularly unlikable to end up coming across as a self-absorbed egomaniac as a result of this POV, and so, care must be taken to avoid alienating the reader even when the POV character is fairly well-balanced or sympathetic.

Of course, the first person POV can also have exactly the opposite effect, and bring readers into outwardly unattractive, unsympathetic, and even boring characters who nonetheless have rich and meaningful insights about and reactions to life and the happenings around them, and sometimes the best tool for such inner journeys is the intimacy that the *I-am* allows. The richness of a character's inner journey may sometimes only be possible to expose and explore by getting under that character's skin in the most inner of points of view.

Compare the following two versions of the same passage, trying to get a sense for which one is more psychically close to the reader:

> Instead of your heartbeat, I hear the detestable tick of powered time as it wastes the seconds of my half-sleep on the wall. The midnight cars of Parc Avenue under my bedroom window sound not like the cars I know they are, but instead like a river that I might have to cross to find you again. Ninety seven. Ninety eight. I tried to imagine that the ticking of the timepiece was not the working of a fourth dimension, but the beating of your heart as I pressed my ear

to it while you slept. Ninety nine. It is not your heart. Can I have counted so high without falling asleep? One hundred. I lose count at a century, brushing my other hand over the edge of the mattress, into oblivion. How many centuries of seconds have I counted off since you left this bed? They have all become one and I cannot remember their number. One. Yes, one. I am alone. Two. How long ago was it that you were with me here?

"Redemption"

Instead of her heartbeat, he hears the detestable tick of powered time as it wastes the seconds of his half-sleep on the wall. The midnight cars of Parc Avenue under his bedroom window sound not like the cars he knows they are, but instead like a river that he might have to cross to find her again. Ninety seven. Ninety eight. He tried to imagine that the ticking of the timepiece was not the working of a fourth dimension, but the beating of her heart as he pressed his ear to it while she slept. Ninety nine. It is not her heart. Can he have counted so high without falling asleep? One hundred. He loses count at a century, brushing his other hand over the edge of the mattress, into oblivion. How many centuries of seconds has he counted off since she left this bed? They have all become one and he cannot remember their number. One. Yes, one. He is alone. Two. How long ago was it that she was with him here?

"Redemption" excerpt, recast into the third person

Consider also this passage from Knut Hamsun's *Hunger*, asking whether or not it would have been as evocative presented in any other POV:

Everything influenced and distracted me; everything I saw made a fresh impression on me. Flies and tiny mosquitoes stick fast to the paper and disturb me. I blow at them to get rid of them—blow harder and harder; to no purpose, the little pests throw themselves on their backs, make themselves heavy, and fight against me until their slender legs bend. They are not to be moved from the spot; they find something to hook on to, set their heels against a comma or an unevenness in the paper, or stand immovably still until they themselves think fit to go their way.

From *Hunger*, Part I

Everything influenced and distracted him; everything he saw made a fresh impression on him. Flies and tiny mosquitoes stick fast to the paper and disturb him. He blows at them to get rid of them—blows harder and harder; to no purpose, the little pests throw themselves on their backs, make themselves heavy, and fight against him until their slender legs bend. They are not to be moved from the spot; they find something to hook on to, set their heels against a comma or an unevenness in the paper, or stand immovably still until they themselves think fit to go their way.

Passage from *Hunger*, recast into the third person

Something—the sense of insanity caused by the protagonist's hunger?—is lost in the second passage. *My* hunger hurts and slowly drives me mad; *his* hunger is a statistic in the morning paper against which I have been anaesthetized by overexposure.

Keep in mind that the first person introduces some artificial boundaries to the narrative that you may find yourself having to work around in awkward ways. If you feel it necessary to the storyline that the reader knows that the narrator's eyes are blue and hair is blond (for instance, if these points are critical to the reader realizing that a witness to a crime could not have possibly seen the narrator at the scene of the crime because the witness describes a brown-eyed brunette to the police), then you must find some not-too-contrived-sounding device to let the reader know the narrator's hair and eye color. Staring into a mirror has been overdone into cliché, and even if we were to wink at this device and allow it, how often do *you* stare into a mirror and say, "I notice my blue eyes and blond hair..."? Were they not that very same color the last five hundred times you looked into the mirror? Why notice them to the point of internal comment now? Having *another* character say, "You have such lovely blue eyes and blond hair," is about as churlish a device. Finding fresh devices to jump old narrative hurdles is all part of what makes writing fiction a challenge, even when we accept that there is nothing new under the sun.

Besides the boundary of physical self-description, boundaries of narrative become important in the first person. Some types of descriptions read as awkward when coming from a first person narrator. Whereas a third person story might be able to pull off the following:

> The couch was old—probably mid-50's in style and color—and made so much noise when people sat down on it that Mrs. Smith upstairs in room 8b would wake with a start.

it is unlikely that a first person narrator could go on about such things without sounding stark raving neurotic.

Of course, if you are *trying* to portray the character as a neurotic detail-minder, this effect may not always be a bad thing. Unreliable, misinformed, self-absorbed, detail-attending narrators who are out of the cosmic information loop of a story can sometimes be very useful tools in the telling of a story, so it may to be the story's advantage to use the first person under some circumstances where it might not otherwise fit. Of course, there is always the device used in such stories as "Jimmy the Fin" that have the first person narrator not be the protagonist, but simply an observer at the edge of the action who is telling someone else's story.

> Best friend I ever had, Jimmy the Fin. He wasn't no Fin, really—we called him that because he had this five dollar bill always hanging over his shirt pocket. Said it was his lucky fin. Lucky. Jimmy was lucky.
>
> Knew Jimmy since we was kids. Did all the usual stuff together: throwing stones, chasing dogs with sticks, climbing trees, kissing the girls and making them cry. Jimmy had a real way with girls. Lucky. Jimmy was lucky with girls.
>
> He started betting the way we all did—on crap shoots. Jimmy could shake those dice, do his lucky magic, and pull up a seven just when it would win him enough money to take us all for a soda. That's sort of what this story I have to tell is about. Not about dice, no, Jimmy grew out of dice and into poker, like the rest of us. He could play any game going, straight faced and tight laced, hours on end. Jimmy had the gift when it came to gambling.
>
> But this is about the time that me and Jimmy was walking for a soda.

"Jimmy the Fin"

THIRD PERSON

If the third person is *third*, why then does it come before the second person in this chapter? For the simple reason that the second person POV is so rare as to warrant later treatment. By far the most common POV is the third person *he* or *she*. The third person can further be divided into the limited and omniscient points of view, with the limitation being whose POV is adhered to throughout the narrative.

In my opinion, it is a rare author who can write an effective third person omniscient short story, given the length requirements of the form, but it does happen from time to time that someone manages to pull it off and the viewpoint can jump back and forth at the author's whim. It can be managed effectively in novels, but for the purposes of the discussion here, I will only cover the limited third person POV.

Once a POV character has been selected, the narration adheres to the principle that it will reveal nothing that this character could not possibly know. The narration is still free to describe things somewhat more freely than one would find in a first person narrative, such as that character's hair and eye color, for instance, but those descriptions are kept within the boundaries of the POV character's knowledge. If this central character knows something, it is a simple matter to throw it into the narrative as needed.

Even so, one will not (or at least *should* not!) find this variation of a Little-Did-He-Know passage in a limited third person narrative:

> Jane did not know it, but the cancer growing within her was already hurting her performance on the job.

It might be tempting for these details to be introduced, but care should be taken to keep the POV as clean as called for by convention, since such passages may instinctively skin the knees of readers and jar them out of the unwritten agreement between an author and reader that says such trickery is out of bounds.♠

The limited third person allows for narrator unreliability, just as with the first person. For instance, if a passage says, "Jane saw a man walking down the street," what the passage might actually mean is, "Jane saw a person *she assumed* to be a man walking down the street" and it may turn out later in the story that Jane actually mistook a woman for a man. Keep this freedom in mind when using this POV, since it may serve you well in surprising a reader without having to resort to smoke and mirrors and other trickery. In other words: just because the limited third person narrative says something happened does not necessarily mean that it happened *exactly* as described or interpreted by the POV character.

SECOND PERSON

When a story is told entirely as if the reader himself (or some imaginary reader over whose shoulder the real reader has magically peered) is the main character of the story, it is in the "pure" second person POV. The primary pronoun used in this form is *you*, though one occasionally spots *we* the way one might in a first person narrative.

This "experimental" POV can be used to great effect, or it can end up reading horribly. Whereas the more traditional first and third person styles are so common that a story has to fail on its own merits when told in those points of view, when a second person narrative fails, it can sometimes do so *just because* of the choice of person, rather than any other flaw of the story.

With that much speaking for it, the frisky author would be well advised to avoid this POV unless it can be

---

♠   For an examination of how far the Little-Did-He-Know concept can be taken, see the movie *Stranger than Fiction*.

supported with a strong rationale. I have dabbled in the second person in short fiction, and sometimes it has worked, while other times it has not met my personal expectations for my own work. For instance, "For a Husband from Shiraz" is told consistently in this POV, and for the most part, the device works therein. I did not select the risky (some might say *risqué*) second person simply because I wanted to litter the story with *yous*, but rather, selected this POV because the protagonist of the story is a woman in a culture where women have very little freedom to openly express their own views. By telling the story in the second person, I felt a certain "bossy"-effect was created; it was as if in such a culture even a story told from the POV of a woman was a call to obedience, since orders are often given in the second person.

In other words, the choice of this device was intended to convey a sense of the woman's powerlessness in her own life in such a social milieu.

You awoke when the cock crew. Your bladder was full and he was kicking it. He was strong and would make a good soldier for Islam, like his father. Bahram was sleeping in the adjoining room, away from you because he did not like the way you tossed and turned in your sleep. You arose, dressed, and waddled into the tiny kitchen to prepare your husband's breakfast. It was then that you noticed that there was no honey, and you knew he would be angry at you for serving his bread without it.

You quickly covered yourself with your *chador* and headed for the market place. The only shop that sold honey would not yet be open, you knew, but you also knew that Bahram would rise soon and that he would demand breakfast as soon as he limped out of his bedroom and saw you. You knew that he would patiently wait for you if you were not there, but would not be so patient with you if you were, and you wanted to avoid another chiding from him.

"For a Husband from Shiraz"

I used the same device in an entirely different degree and context and for different reasons in the short story "Stand-In." In "Stand-In," the main narration actually occurs in what would mostly be called the first person, but in the first half of the story, the narrator directly addresses the focus of his affection so often in the second person that the story almost reads as if it begins as a second person narrative.

This is not the "pure" second person POV, but shares some elements with it.

> I thought I saw you walk by the storefront as I stood at the back, snapping shirtsleeves straight in the steam of the maiden. Part of me, the reasonable part, knew it could not possibly be you, since you were half a world away, but I wanted to let loose my grip, run to the front door, look out, and be certain. The reasonable part of me won, and I stayed to my task, forgetting to lift my foot in time, scalding my right hand in the blast. At first, I did not feel the wound, but as I pulled off the shirt to put another one on the mannequin, I began to notice the searing in my wrist. I walked over to the sink, turned on the cold water, and put my hand under the stream.

"Stand-In"

EXPERIMENTAL POINTS OF VIEW

One might think the second person POV is experimental enough a viewpoint that the daring author need not stretch his creative fingers any further than that. Not so; other possibilities exist.

For instance, the POV character need not be human, or even sentient. One chapter of *Abadoun*, while technically written in the second person, the *you* involved is an innkeeper's cat.

> High above Master you stretch in slumber as he sorts his things at the small table in front him. You will jump on his table when he is not looking up at you and sprawl out to scatter his things once more.
>
> The front door of the caravanserai opens and you quickly decide that you want to stay inside where it is warm, since you can feel the briskness of the night air on your old, wet nose and it is not inviting. The Smelly One comes in and approaches Master with his hand outstretched.

"Jafar!" he calls out. Master grasps his hand and smiles the way he does with you after having tossed you some meat. "How are you, old man?"

"I am doing well, Abdul," Master says. "It has been slow, but I've got two rooms let for the night. I can't hope for more than that these days, you know."

The Smelly One nods his head like a rat sniffing about for food scraps. "Travelers, then? Got some travelers bedding down for the night, do we? They usually go on to Baneh for the night."

"I suppose so. Most of them *are* travelers. Not too many villagers come here, unless their roofs are rained out, or something. I don't ask too many questions when they finally do wander into this place."

"Yeah, not too many questions to scare them away, I guess. Don't want to scare them away, hey? Not paying customers, anyway."

"You got it. It's certainly not like when *Kaak* Abadlou ran this place as a guest house to show everyone how *hospitable* he was to strangers." Master sits down on his stool and offers the Smelly One a cup of some steaming tea.

From *Abadoun*, Chapter 4

If one might argue, in some worldview, that a cat is sentient, it is possible to go a step further, as another chapter of *Abadoun* is written from the POV of a bowl hanging on a wall.

High on the wall it hangs at *Peiman-e-Omar*, overlooking the main room of the small coffeehouse. It is cracked at places along its lip. Deep at its glazed bottom hunts a forgotten nobleman, spear held high, ready to deliver the *coup de grâce* to the wounded boar, but never releasing to claim the kill. The voices that fill the room echo clearly through it—it hears everything.

As has always been so at daybreak, it hears the bolt of the back door being thrown vigorously open by Omar, owner of the coffeehouse. Minutes pass before he comes out of the back room and into sight of the bowl. It sees him readying the place for customers. He then disappears again for a while and the boy comes out. This is all as it always has been.

The boy passes in front of it and looks closely at the hunter, holding up his broom in imitation of the hunter.

"Playing again?" comes Omar's voice from the shadows. "Get to work, boy!"

From *Abadoun*, Chapter 14

It is even possible, at least for short passages, that the narrative have no discernible POV at all, as is the case in "Soldiers' Sisters."

"Who is she?"

Photograph of veiled woman in shivering hand of the Islamic Revolutionary Guard. Quick glance over to the direction of the voice. His reply: "My sister."

Bowing of heads among the other eleven. Understanding without words. Noise from stones under the wheels of the vehicle piercing everyone's ears. Bouncing and bowing. Memories of other sisters and fiancees. Some prayers and supplications.

"She's getting married this spring."

Nods and smiles. Hands on rifles, hands holding scarves to young, fearful faces. Bouncing bodies, close together. Gasps from the bouncing and prayers for the betrothed.

"Married. That's *good*. My sister will be happy with him. He's a good man." *Pasdar's* words. Listening ears.

"Married to a good man. Yeah, that's wonderful." Words said to please *pasdar's* ears.

Memories of his sister jumping about with the jerking of the bench. Memories of warmer days at the edges of Teheran. Memories of daylight and of smiling, uncovered faces. Memories of candies shipped fresh from Esfahan especially for *Nouruz* festivals and of sweet, sticky *zulbia* at other weddings.

"Soldiers' Sisters"

The narrative of this story contains no verbs, and thus, a certain universality is established by such phrases as "nods and smiles." Who nods, who smiles, and who observes either? It is not important: these soldiers are all in the same truck, all fighting for the same reason, all at the same risk of being killed in battle. In this sense, the story is told from every character's viewpoint, simultaneously.

The lack of a specific POV becomes more clear at the end of the story:

Silence. Obeying orders. Bouncing and praying. Loud cracking bursts and sudden motion in circles. Legs and arms all interwoven. From the driver: "A tire's been shot out!"

Dread. Fear. Panic. Noise.

"Sir? Orders?"

"Return fire!" from the young one.

"Kurds!" from the older soldier. Rifles aimed at the hills, safeties off, ready to kill.

"Can't see 'em!" from the driver.

Pasdar's order: "Shoot at will! To kill!"

Random shots back and forth. Screaming soldier at his side, hit in the left shoulder, pouring out blood and oaths.

Pasdar to driver: "Can we get out of here?"

"Won't turn over."

Sound of rocks and road beneath *pasdar's* boots on side of truck opposite the hills and Kurds. Quick steps to the front of the truck. Finger on trigger, rifle up, firing over the front end of the truck. Echoes of bullets hitting only stone.

Pain of bullet tearing into his neck, knocking him off his feet. Spinning. Warmth of his blood pouring from him and down his collar. Desperation in his actions. Hands digging in his shirt for the photograph.

Screaming and joyousness from the young one: "I got one! My first kill! Allah be praised—I killed one of the Kurds!"

Fingers almost tearing the photograph. Eyes wanting to close, ears wanting to close. Head back on the stones of the road. Pain disappearing. Light disappearing.

"Sir?" coming from the driver. "Sir? Oh my God! Two men to help me!"

Blackness approaching. Photograph pressed to his bloody lips for a last kiss from sister. Nineteen year old *pasdar*, defender of the faith.

And in Teheran, a Shi'ite sister rending her shawl.

"Soldiers' Sisters"

Tense and the Passage of Time

"What a funny watch!" she remarked. "It tells the day of the month, and doesn't tell what o'clock it is!"

"Why should it?" muttered the Hatter. "Does *your* watch tell you what year it is?"

"Of course not," Alice replied very readily: "but that's because it stays the same year for such a long time together."

"Which is just the case with *mine*," said the Hatter.

—Lewis Carroll, *Alice in Wonderland*

The tense in which you choose to write a story will have some impact on how the story is perceived by the reader, and how effectively you will be able to negotiate the passing of time in the story. By far the most common tense is the past tense, followed in popularity by the present tense. I have yet to see a work written fully in the future tense, but there is no reason it could not be done by an author with enough skill and pluck.

THE LITERARY PAST

When we speak of a story being in the past, we really mean that it is in a past relative to the time of the narration. A story about someone in A.D. 2050 can be told as if it were in a foggy, distant past.

Technically, the past tense used in most fiction is known as the *simple* past. This is the form of such verbs as *said, did, loved, hated,* and so on—each action described is wholly and fully (simply) completed. When one wishes to speak of events that occur in the past relative to the past of the narrative itself, one is left with the sometimes awkward tense the French call the *plus-que-parfait*—the more than perfect tense, the pluperfect (or past perfect), such as in the following passage:

> It **had been** in a similar place to the east, at a similar antique oasis village that Manning Berithson and his wife Lilith **had uncovered** the golden coffer. How long they **had been** in Kaloun at the dig he could not remember, for the two **had almost given up** all hope of uncovering anything other than the bones of the unimportant dead in the ancient *gabbana* that was to the south of the village. But when things looked the bleakest they had in months, Lilith's spade did not go into the ground in the way a seasoned archeologist knew it should.

"Charon's Fee"

You will notice the shift into the pluperfect, and then the gradual return to the simple past once the timeline of the flashback has been established. It is very difficult to pull off the pluperfect for more than a few sentences without the prose becoming awkward. After all, when we speak of events long since past, we rarely maintain the pluperfect in speech for more than a sentence or two.

The literary past can also be the repetitious past. Consider this excerpt from Maugham's *Of Human Bondage*, where Maugham has created a sense of routine and repetition with the careful use of such phrases as "would feel" and "often they did not talk" and "she would never acknowledge" and "every now and then." It is difficult to tell whether or not the passage represents a single such incident, or a repetitious event:

> For the next three months Philip went every day to see Mildred. He took his books with him and after tea worked, while Mildred lay on the sofa reading novels. Sometimes he would look up and watch her for a minute. A happy smile crossed his lips. She would feel his eyes upon her.
>
> "Don't waste your time looking at me, silly. Go on with your work," she said.
>
> "Tyrant," he answered gaily.
>
> He put aside his book when the landlady came in to lay the cloth for dinner, and in his high spirits he exchanged chaff with her.

She was a little cockney, of middle age, with an amusing humour and a quick tongue. Mildred had become great friends with her and had given her an elaborate but mendacious account of the circumstances which had brought her to the pass she was in. The good-hearted little woman was touched and found no trouble too great to make Mildred comfortable. Mildred's sense of propriety had suggested that Philip should pass himself off as her brother. They dined together, and Philip was delighted when he had ordered something which tempted Mildred's capricious appetite. It enchanted him to see her sitting opposite him, and every now and then from sheer joy he took her hand and pressed it. After dinner she sat in the arm-chair by the fire, and he settled himself down on the floor beside her, leaning against her knees, and smoked. Often they did not talk at all, and sometimes Philip noticed that she had fallen into a doze. He dared not move then in case he woke her, and he sat very quietly, looking lazily into the fire and enjoying his happiness.

"Had a nice little nap?" he smiled, when she woke.

"I've not been sleeping," she answered. "I only just closed my eyes."

She would never acknowledge that she had been asleep.

From *Of Human Bondage*, Chapter 72

THE LITERARY PRESENT

Stories told in the literary present tense can drift into the past tense when, indeed, the events being narrated occurred in the past relative to the narrative present. (How's that for a complicated sentence?) This removes the need for the awkward pluperfect tense altogether, since that would be plu-pluperfect tense (e.g. "he had had been") in a past tense narrative, and this is not something that crops up in real story telling.

It is not difficult to end up sounding silly in the present tense, so I suggest caution when using it. Statements such as "John is standing in front of Bob, shooting into the air, flailing his left arm about like a little Mussolini," just *sound* odd—like something one might see in Charlie Chaplin's movie *The Great Dictator*.

Narrative that mixes the first person present with passages of stream of consciousness can be used to effect where the same passages, written in the past tense, might come across as somewhat contrived. Compare these two versions of the same passage from "Redemption," for instance:

My leg falls over the side of the bed and the bottom of my foot barely touches the hardwood floor. It is cold, and brings my eyes open. Overhead are the slowly moving cast eye shadows of street lights, car head light ricochets. Or is that really a river? The roof shimmers like the surface of a lake under a midnight moon. But your departure has brought me a new moon—those are headlights.

"Redemption"

My leg fell over the side of the bed and the bottom of my foot barely touched the hardwood floor. It was cold, and brought my eyes open. Overhead were the slowly moving cast eye shadows of street lights, car head light ricochets. Or was that really a river? The roof shimmered like the surface of a lake under a midnight moon. But your departure had brought me a new moon—those were headlights.

"Redemption" excerpt, recast into the past tense

The first version (as it was published) is immediate, and the asides in the mind of the narrator flow naturally. Cast into the past tense, the asides come across as being corny (to me, anyway) ... sort of like a character in a play, dead on the ground with a knife in his chest, spouting out, "Woe is me, for I am dead!"

EXPERIMENTAL TENSES

As already mentioned in the section on points of view, the narrative of the short story "Soldiers' Sisters" contains no verbs. Since (in English, at least), tense is conveyed mostly through verb conjugation, the story, like the Mad Hatter's watch, "doesn't tell what o'clock it is." It follows

31

that this story, in addition to having no discernable POV, has no discernable tense. Whether this reflects the immediate now, or the timeless forever, I shall let the reader decide.

It might also be considered "experimental" for tense to shift quickly. Consider again this passage from Hamsun's *Hunger*:

> Everything influenced and distracted me; everything I saw made a fresh impression on me. Flies and tiny mosquitoes stick fast to the paper and disturb me. I blow at them to get rid of them—blow harder and harder; to no purpose, the little pests throw themselves on their backs, make themselves heavy, and fight against me until their slender legs bend. They are not to be moved from the spot; they find something to hook on to, set their heels against a comma or an unevenness in the paper, or stand immovably still until they themselves think fit to go their way.

From *Hunger*, Part I

The shifts of tense ("stick fast" rather than "stuck fast") create an immediacy that bring the reader into the narrator's deteriorating state of mind. Tense, like sanity, need not remain static.

Setting the Scene

Of all the strange things that Alice saw in her journey Through the Looking-Glass, this was the one that she always remembered most clearly. Years afterwards she could bring the whole scene back again, as if it had been only yesterday— the mild blue eyes and kindly smile of the Knight—the setting sun gleaming through his hair, and shining on his armour in a blaze of light that quite dazzled her—the horse quietly moving about, with the reins hanging loose on his neck, cropping the grass at her feet—and the black shadows of the forest behind—all this she took in like a picture, as, with one hand shading her eyes, she leant against a tree, watching the strange pair, and listening, in a half-dream, to the melancholy music of the song.

—Lewis Carroll, *Through the Looking-Glass*

Fiction can take you anywhere. Imagine being able to visit an Italian count's castle in the Nineteenth Century, the estate of a New York art patron, a post-Spanish Civil War villa near Pamplona, a rural town in Iranian Kurdistan, the Vancouver Seawall, the Seine in Paris, a Buddhist temple in the mountains of Northern India, an abandoned dance studio in the woods off Dijon, a logging camp on a small island on the West Coast of British Columbia, a library in Cambridge University, a penthouse apartment and courthouse in an unnamed city, a private investigator's office in London, a university in Philadelphia, a San Francisco jazz bar, a coffee shop in Montreal, parts unknown of Saudi Arabia, and the city of the dead in the afterlife, all in the span of fifteen years. These are but a few of the places visited in my fiction written since the early 1990's.

Not counting the time shifts, I have only had personal experience with three of the above settings: having grown up in Vancouver, Canada, I have walked along the Vancouver Seawall many times. I also lived on a small island off the West Coast of British Columbia, and once ate lunch in a Montreal jazz bar. All the other locales are pure fantasy, speculation, and attentive listening when those who *have* been in other places have told me about them, but I did not let that stop me from setting stories in those places and times. Fiction provides safe, cheap mind and time travel, with no risk of jet lag.

Setting is an important part of all fiction, short or long, but because of space constraints the short story form place upon the writer, it is not always possible to describe settings in very much detail, except where absolutely necessary for the movement of the story. For this reason, the author of short fiction learns a few shortcuts in setting up a scene. He learns the art of making what novelist Patricia C. Wrede calls the "soap-bubble illusion."

As you read the paragraph of "Master D'Arcy's Protégée," try to spot the devices used to help in setting up the scene:

> After carefully placing her torn slippers into her rucksack and strapping the sack to herself, Elvire Beauregard left her small bedroom to bid her mother good-bye. Georgine Beauregard, Elvire's aging mother, kissed first her right and then her left cheek. She did not need to ask her daughter where she planned to go with the rucksack because she believed that Elvire had the habit of visiting the library in Dijon. She often had declared that the bicycle ride into the city was a bit too far for a young girl to manage every day, but allowed her to venture there after returning from school. The reading sessions seemed to be bringing the previously depressive girl into the light of day, and Madame Beauregard did not wish to interfere with a good thing.

"Master D'Arcy's Protégée"

There is a good deal of setting information in the opening of "Protégée," worked into the whole of the paragraph. The first hint that the story is about a young dancer comes from the introduction of *torn slippers*. Next, we are introduced to the non-English names of the protagonist and her mother, and the French custom of kissing both cheeks when greeting or bidding someone good-bye. Then, we are given a hint that Elvire has been deceiving her mother about her comings and goings in the phrase "she believed Elvire had the habit of...." Those readers who did not know that Dijon is a city in France, probably realize this by the end of the first paragraph, given the title "Madame" and other markers of "foreignness." Finally, we are told that Elvire's mother has been granting her daughter concessions for some reason. All of these setting details are brought to bear on the story while the story's action begins, without interrupting the flow of the primary action: Elvire is heading out on her bicycle to do something her mother does not know about.

The next three paragraphs of the story, then, come as no surprise, since the reader has already been primed:

> Young Mademoiselle Beauregard would take her bicycle down the road, but instead of continuing past the overgrown pathway that branched almost unnoticed off the main road, she would chain her bicycle to a tree near the path. How she had first noticed the path she could no longer remember, for it appeared a mere dent in the thick growth at the edge of the road. But when one started down the path, one saw that it grew less overgrown, until it became as if much frequented. It had been one month after the death of her father, Jean-Paul Beauregard that she, in a particularly somber mood, decided to continue down the trail until she discovered its goal and purpose. That day she had discovered the abandoned dance studio.
>
> On this day, after being sent off by her unsuspecting mother, Elvire rode to the path as she had been doing during the six months since she had found the old building. She knew that her mother believed her lie about going to the library in Dijon, and felt confident that her secret would never be discovered. As she glided down the path, she recalled to herself how she had met the old man six months before.
>
> Upon finally arriving at the old wooden building, Elvire removed her slippers from the rucksack, undid her heavy coat, and entered the musty air of the place. This ritual she had repeated many times since the death of her father, always in the same order and with the same feeling of anticipation. Her efforts would always be rewarded when she heard the voice of the old dance instructor coming from its place in the shadowy north corner of the large practice room.

"Master D'Arcy's Protégée"

At no point (I hope!) is the reader flooded with too many setting details than are needed to tell the story effectively.

The story "In the Shadow of Clay Pigeons" is one of my few that is set somewhere (and within an age frame) I have actually been, and begins as follows:

> Summer days in the logging camp passed slowly through the horsefly-ridden heat. On Saturday nights, there were the radio plays that managed to bounce from the States, all the way up to Maple Bay on Guilford Island. *The Shadow* and *The Whistler* came across time and space to Mark's radio, as he hid under his blanket with his ear pressed against the speaker so his stepfather wouldn't hear him. To Mark, the only child in the camp since his arrival a year earlier, these may as well have been live productions, since they were the only entertainment he had. When two of the married men of the camp moved in their families from the Vancouver mainland, then, Mark was more than happy to have some company.

"In the Shadow of Clay Pigeons"

The first six words of the story set up the time and place, and the second half of the first sentence gives some feeling for the place. Next, we are shown the protagonist's isolation from other children, and some of the coping mechanisms he has created to deal with his loneliness.

In "When a Stranger Wandered In," the general setting is established within the span of the first two paragraphs of the story:

> There was no work for outsiders in Thornburn. Whatever such work there might have been had long since moved away. No one had bought or sold a house there in at least a generation. When a stranger wandered into town, it got him noticed. If he wasn't just passing through, he always ended up at *The Old Door*, the only place to rent a room. Keith Coppersmith, the owner of the inn, would then pass the information on to the regulars at his bar, and within a day, the speculation began over at the drug store and the barbershop. Most often, by the time the speculation started to get exaggerated, the stranger was gone and it didn't matter anymore, but every now and again he'd stay on longer than most, and the real

sport of gossip would get going. The tall, slender guest at the inn had already been there for three weeks, always paid each week in advance in cash, and had not said a word to anyone about what his business in the town was or when he planned to move on. In the Thornburn system, that had elevated him to the kind of celebrity status very few managed to achieve.

Every morning at ten o'clock, he came out of his single bed room, ate a small breakfast of ham and eggs with a black coffee, put back one glass of milk, and returned to his room until two o'clock. At two, he came down for a corned beef on rye, and then wandered out onto the many trails in the groves around the town, some which led to the river, and others which led to the old mining shacks. Around six every night, he returned, had a small supper, and returned to his room.

"When a Stranger Wandered In"

It is not until later in the story, however, that the *era* of the narrative (that is, post World War Two America) and the true nature of the narrator's background are made clear:

"So the mystery visitor has a name," Anna said as she directed him to the dining room. "You have created quite a stir in Thornburn," she then admitted. "Would you like some coffee or tea?"

"Coffee would be nice, thank you," he said. "Black. I can't imagine how I could have created a 'stir', Ma'am."

"Anna Macdonald," she greeted as she put the coffee pot on the stove. "Oh, Mr. Lafontaine, you haven't created a stir by *doing* anything unseemly. You have to understand how a town like Thornburn works. We're just a little piece of America. We have our mysteries and our secrets, and we like to amuse ourselves by pretending that anyone who comes through longer than a few days is some great unexplained threat or salvation. I suppose," she added as she put the coffee cup on its saucer, "it's how we keep ourselves from losing our heads in this place. It changes so little from year to year."

Adrian sat at her table, his back straight. "Oh, I understand Mrs. Macdonald," he said. "Before my time in Europe, I lived in a small town not unlike Thornburn."

"You lived in Europe?" Anna asked. She reached for the pie on the window, cut out a piece, and put it on her best plate.

"I served in France," Adrian replied.

Anna smiled. "Oh, I see. Which branch was that, Mr. Lafontaine?"

"The United States Marine Corps, Ma'am."

"When a Stranger Wandered In"

In fact, much of "When a Stranger Wandered In" sets the scene for the final movement of the final few paragraphs of the story. What Adrian Lafontaine has to say—his very reason for staying in town and wandering about looking at the landscape for so long without really making a point of explaining his purpose for being in Thornburn—only fully makes sense when the entire scene has been set. Lafontaine has been looking for a place that is the "same" as his hometown, but populated by strangers. Setting, then, is everything.

Without a full establishment of time, place, and atmosphere, his final speech to Coppersmith the innkeeper has much less meaning:

Adrian took a long sip from his beer and finally said, "You might think I'm a stranger to your little town, but I grew up in a town not unlike this. Names were different, is all. Same air. Same dust on the road. Same barbershop. Same post office. Same kind of picnics after church. You understand?"

"It's a good, quiet life."

Adrian put his hand again on the innkeeper's shoulder. "But you see, sir, when you go away … and see so much … so much death and destruction, it changes you. Inside. It changes your eyes. You can look in my eyes, and it won't matter, you understand? It won't matter to you, because you're a stranger. You never knew me before I went to war. Someone like Susan Brown can look into my eyes, and maybe take a fancy to me. Maybe want me to ask her to dance."

"Supposing you're properly introduced," Mr. Coppersmith said, poking Adrian in the ribs lightly and grinning.

"Yes. Supposing we're properly introduced," he agreed, grinning back. "Mrs. Trent and Mrs. Macdonald can look into these eyes and see a decent young man who served his country and came back alive in mostly working order. A stranger with an honorable past and a decent idea for the future. But nobody over in Willowbrook, my hometown, can do that now. They remember the old eyes. The eyes that never looked into a dying man's face and shoved the bayonet a little harder. The eyes that never saw someone all of sixteen years of age die three feet from them. You understand? They can't look into these eyes, and I can't look into theirs. Not anymore. It's cold and it's chilling. You understand? Like you've never felt, I assure you.

"A stranger wandered into my body when I went over there to fight, you understand? A stranger that none of them recognize anymore, and who doesn't recognize them. But I can look into strangers' eyes, and they mine, because they never knew me before. They don't know what color they were before they went different from all that. I still remember what I loved about the small town life. That the bastards couldn't steal from me. So I want that back. That little piece of apple pie they couldn't steal from me. I can build from there."

"When a Stranger Wandered In"

Plot & Movement

This piece of rudeness was more than Alice could bear: she got up in great disgust, and walked off; the Dormouse fell asleep instantly, and neither of the others took the least notice of her going, though she looked back once or twice, half hoping that they would call after her: the last time she saw them, they were trying to put the Dormouse into the teapot.

"At any rate I'll never go *there* again!" said Alice as she picked her way through the wood. "It's the stupidest tea-party I ever was at in all my life!"

—Lewis Carroll, *Alice in Wonderland*

Plot is more than moving from point A to B in a story, but is rather the entire *structure* of a story in terms of action, inaction, and how that structure plays a role in moving (or being moved by, or *failing* to be moved by) the characters of the story. Nothing seems random in real life, if you seek structure, so perhaps structure in fiction is the author's statement of such a belief in the underlying form of life and its many events. Not "the story must be random because life is random" but "fiction requires structure because the examined life has an underlying structure."

Although some books on writing will speak of beginnings, middles, and endings, with a dramatic climax and subsequent denouement somewhere along the way, it is not entirely true to say that every narrative has a beginning, middle, and ending, in the proper senses of each of these concepts. In the story "Fractures," for instance, a Muslim man awakes, says his morning prayer, goes out onto his porch to gather a care package left by a local boy, and then sits down with his cat. Even if we grant that "waking up in the morning" constitutes some sort of beginning, where are the monumentally distinct middle and ending of that scenario?

Even a piece with no real demarcation of beginning, middle, and ending can show human movement, however. Consider this excerpt from the short story "Fractures":

Ahmet tickled under Gris' chin a bit as he pulled one wedge of the orange at a time from the first half. The tips of his fingers could feel the shaking of her purr. "You can't eat oranges," he apologized to her. "Maybe if he had brought a banana like yesterday," he then tried to explain to his cat. Gris didn't seem to care at all that she would go without a snack; the sound of her claws scraping happily on the wooden floor seemed to say that she wanted her chin scratched, and nothing more.

"You know, Gris, if someone wanted to poison me, all they would have to do is figure out that Mahmet leaves a piece of fruit for me every morning. I'd be easy to poison. Creature of habit. Full of fractures."

Gris didn't care. She just scratched the floor under her claws, pushed her nose into Ahmet Bey's callused hand, and accepted what she could get.

"Fractures"

At the point that Ahmet Bey realizes he is dead to the world because he has become a "creature of habit," his realization that he will not move forward is the climax of human movement of the story, and the "end" of both the story and Ahmet Bey's effective life arrives.

That said, many pieces (particularly novels) *do* have a (more or less) distinct beginning, middle, and ending, and so I will discuss each of these.

BEGINNINGS

As already mentioned under the chapter entitled "Setting the Scene," the beginning of a piece can often be used to frame the story about to be told. Beginnings are covered herein under two different headings for the simple reason that they are so important, especially in short fiction, since, given the brevity of short stories, the beginning is usually the most effective place to catch the reader's immediate interest and introduce the main tone of the story.

Consider how the beginning of "Elspeth Stood at the Edge" immediately introduces the main conflict of the story:

> Elspeth stood at the edge, her toes over the side of the seawall as the water sprayed up to her uncovered knees, unable to hear her own thoughts over the crash of the sea. The cold pinched her toes, which were now wet even through her shoes, and her nostrils stung, but since her hands were in her overcoat pockets, they did not hurt. Tears had once stung her eyes, too, but they were gone now, and only spray and rain soaked her face.
>
> Elspeth stood at the edge, waiting for the wind to change direction, so that it would be at her back, so that it would shove her off, and she would not have to gather the strength to jump. But the wind did not change direction, and continued to blow against her, almost pulling her hair in a straight line behind her head. One change in the wind would tell her that everything was for her decision, and nothing against it, but the wind did not agree with her as she stood, trying to convince it.

"Elspeth Stood at the Edge"

As can be ascertained from the first two paragraphs of "Elspeth," the protagonist is about to attempt suicide. Within a few sentences of the start of the story, the reader is brought right to the edge of this young woman's crisis.

Another, less dramatic beginning that nonetheless introduces the main conflict of the story, comes from the opening paragraphs of "Two Brothers":

> Even good water wouldn't go down Mahmoud Zamani's throat. That's what his brother Reza always told him. But Reza was always finding something critical to say about Mahmoud, the younger of the two.
>
> "Ever since we came here, you've lived a dog's life," Reza would say.
>
> "We did not came here, Dadash," Mahmoud would always reply. "We are refugees. They send us here."

"Two Brothers"

42

This beginning introduces the continuing conflict between the brothers Reza and Mahmoud Zamani, as well as a hint at the ideological cause of their struggles. The use of the phrases "would say" and "would always reply," indicates that these two brothers have long been at one another's throats.

Beginnings can startle a reader into interest beyond simply having a young woman standing on a ledge, ready to jump:

It was three days going before Todd Schmidt realized he was dead. Were it not for his loss of appetite, and for the smell of his own rotting flesh nearly causing him to pass out when he sniffed under his arms, he may not have even noticed. It was a good thing, then, that he worked outdoors, alone and starting at eleven o'clock nights, without anyone around the gas pump islands to notice. Besides, death was easy enough to work around, once he set his mind to learning a few useful habits, like brushing only the enamel of his teeth, rather than his gums, so that he wouldn't end up rinsing pieces of his former self down the sink. He had to lose a tooth to figure out the necessity of this new habit, but once he had his pattern down, it began to come easy.

"Raven Shift"

The fact that the protagonist of "Raven Shift" has been dead for some time is obviously the startling beginning (ending?) to which I am referring.

Another device that can sometimes be used to catch a reader's eye is a catchy bit of dialog that is taken out of context:

"Only if you smoke menthols," Nick replied as he shoved aside his highball and turned to face her.

When she offered her hand, he flipped out his pack and gave her a cigarette. "Anything in a pinch," she said, sitting beside him.

Nick turned back to his drink and took another sip as she lit up. When only ice remained, he shook the tumbler in the direction of the bartender to indicate he wanted another. Since he had the pack out, he took out a cigarette for himself and lit up one of his own.

"Apartment"

It is clear only after reading a few sentences beyond the opening statement by Nick that the woman has asked if she can have one of his cigarettes. The shock that having a conversation begin in midstream creates has been used repeatedly in fiction.

MIDDLES

Please do not think me facetious when I say that the "middle" of a piece is everything that is neither the beginning or the ending, but I can think of no simpler way of expressing it. The point at which the beginning of a story becomes the middle depends entirely on the story in question. In some stories, this point will come as quickly as the second paragraph—in others, it may take a few pages. In yet others, it may not come until right near the end.

Once a setting has been laid out and the reader has somehow been made aware of the issues that must be resolved before movement can be seen to take place, the middle of the story takes over. Most of the conflict of a story, whether internal or external, takes place at this time.

The middle of a work need not be the longest of the three parts. A conflict can take some time to introduce, but then come to a fairly speedy resolution, as in the story "Washed Up," wherein the protagonist's apathy about his current lifestyle is slowly introduced throughout the story, and his final recognition of his apathy ties up the story in the last few short paragraphs.

ENDINGS

I consider the ending of a piece to be its most important (and most vulnerable) architectural feature. The most excellently executed piece, no matter how it begins and is carried through, if it ends poorly, will likely be remembered only for the last awful passages read. I firmly believe that with fiction, last impressions matter more than first impressions. In many of my works, I try to tie the ending in with the beginning in some tangible way, while at the same time providing the required closure.

Consider the first and last paragraphs of "Two Brothers," for instance:

> Even good water wouldn't go down Mahmoud Zamani's throat. That's what his brother Reza always told him. But Reza was always finding something critical to say about Mahmoud, the younger of the two.
>
> [...]
>
> He lifted a glass of German wine to his lip, and tried to smile at his girlfriend, but Mahmoud's empty seat almost glared at him, and he felt too awkward to take a sip. Even good water wouldn't go down Reza Zamani's throat.

"Two Brothers"

A similar effect is created in "Elspeth Stood at the Edge," which has Elspeth ready to jump in the opening paragraphs and clinging to life with all her might in the closing paragraph:

> Elspeth stood at the edge, her toes over the side of the seawall as the water sprayed up to her uncovered knees, unable to hear her own thoughts over the crash of the sea. The cold pinched her toes, which were now wet even through her shoes, and her nostrils stung, but since her hands were in her overcoat pockets, they did not hurt. Tears had once stung her eyes, too, but they were gone now, and only spray and rain soaked her face.
>
> Elspeth stood at the edge, waiting for the wind to change direction, so that it would be at her back, so that it would shove her off, and she would not have to gather the strength to jump.
>
> [...]
>
> Elspeth clung to the edge, coughing up sea water, her body completely numb under the water as the waves pounded her against the slimy surface of the rocks, her arm hooked over the six inch rock ledge. Connor Swift stood in the shadows, only feet away, cold and waiting for the wind to change direction.

"Elspeth Stood at the Edge"

Endings need not directly echo beginnings to emphasize a point. They may, instead, simply tie the key points together neatly for the reader.

Consider the closing paragraphs of "Paladin," a story wherein one man betrays his best friend by sleeping with his wife:

> "If it had been anyone but you, Benny," Drake said, taking a deep drag from his smoke, "I'd have decked you. It *was* you, though. Benny, don't you know what power you have over people? I'll learn to live with this. It's all part of the ebb and flow."
>
> "What am I, charmed?" Cohen smiled at his friend.
>
> "Must be," Drake replied, blowing circles out into the cold New York wind.
>
> Cohen put his own arm around Drake's back and started to laugh. At the very depths of where he allowed himself to question what he meant, he tried to stand back and see a hero or a villain, but could only see two drunken idiots standing on a balcony, throwing butts into the wind, some blowing left, some right.

"Paladin"

The above ending shows the reader that Drake and Cohen Benjamin are to remain friends, even after Cohen's betrayal of Drake's trust. The cigarette butts' blowing to both the left and right is symbolic of the balance that has been retained in their relationship.

Another story that uses the same approach (that is, tying up loose ends as neatly as can be done without overdoing it) is "Anders' Contrition." The protagonist's wife has died, and the story follows his slow path to acceptance. Earlier in the story, Anders' priest has told him to pray the rosary and give everything he can to the poor, to help him forgive himself for the argument that led to his wife's accidental death. Anders has already given all he can to the poor, but by the end of the story, has not yet prayed the rosary. This he symbolically does in the closing paragraphs of the story:

> "Let's go back inside for some dessert, Anders," Gary finally suggested.
>
> "I think I'll stay out here and listen to the silence, if you don't mind," Anders replied.

Gary placed his right hand on Anders' left shoulder, saying nothing. Soon, he lifted his hand, turned, and went back into the house. Anders sucked the cold air of Christmas Day into his chest and listened only to his own breathing and to the words of the Our Fathers and Hail Marys that constantly repeated themselves in his head as he moved his stare from one house's window to the next. He hadn't owned a rosary for fifteen years, so the panes of windows and the outdoor lights of Christmas would have to suffice.

"Anders' Contrition"

Novels can be particularly tricky to end, even when tricks of time and space allow us as authors to begin at the end and end at the beginning.

Probably the most influential novel ending I have ever been personally affected by is the ending to Jack London's semi-autobiographical novel, *Martin Eden*:

His wilful hands and feet began to beat and churn about, spasmodically and feebly. But he had fooled them and the will to live that made them beat and churn. He was too deep down. They could never bring him to the surface. He seemed floating languidly in a sea of dreamy vision. Colors and radiances surrounded him and bathed him and pervaded him. What was that? It seemed a lighthouse; but it was inside his brain—a flashing, bright white light. It flashed swifter and swifter. There was a long rumble of sound, and it seemed to him that he was falling down a vast and interminable stairway. And somewhere at the bottom he fell into darkness. That much he knew. He had fallen into darkness. And at the instant he knew, he ceased to know.

Last Paragraph of *Martin Eden*

Writing an ending like *that* takes brass ones as a writer. Why so? First, the passage is in the third person, and well, the protagonist up and dies on us. London could have chosen to play around and go on for one more sentence with some commentary, since clearly the third person omniscient POV is being employed. Instead, despite his flair with words and his flamboyance (bordering on verbosity!) in other parts of the same novel, he just up and quits and lets *he ceased to know* stare the reader down.

Martin Eden (the character) is "finished" and so is *Martin Eden* (the novel). Period.

Dialog

"Speak when you're spoken to!" the Queen sharply interrupted her.

"But if everybody obeyed that rule," said Alice, who was always ready for a little argument, "and if you only spoke when you were spoken to, and the other person always waited for *you* to begin, you see nobody would ever say anything, so that—"

"Ridiculous!" cried the Queen.

—Lewis Carroll, *Through the Looking-Glass*

People talk. All the time. And they don't talk the way they write. Rarely, anyway.

If dialog is to capture the way people really talk, and at the same time contribute to the whole of the piece, the author is greatly aided if he does not have a tin ear. Educated characters may not often utter words like *ain't*, but they are not likely to spout out filibusters littered with semicolons either, and uneducated characters, although their speech may be peppered with *ain'ts*, still have a point to make as part of the flow of a story, and have to be kept under as much control as their more educated counterparts. And then there are the speakers who fall somewhere into the murky in-between.

Rather than offering suggestions on how to write dialog, I will offer some suggestions on how to listen to other people when they talk. It can be painfully difficult to analyze speech patterns when one is actively involved in the conversation under analysis, so I am not suggesting trying to figure out how someone to whom you are speaking turns his phrases. First, listen to *other people* when they talk. (Just do not jot down notes while listening, or they will quickly shut their mouths and you may end up with a black eye.)

As you listen to others, ask yourself a few questions about the conversation. What do they seem to be *trying* to say? Are they getting their points across effectively? Do others appear to really be listening, or do replies come back prepackaged without any consideration for what has already actually been said? How long are the sentences in the back-and-forth? Any speeches taking place? You will probably hear a lot of appropriate places to place a comma, an em-dash, ellipses, a full stop, a question mark, and an occasional exclamation point, but do you "hear" many openings for colons or semicolons?

Besides the content and form of what they are saying, what do people *do* when they are speaking with (or *at*) one another? Do they stand back, move forward, smile, pull their lips up to bare their teeth, lean on their hands? And on the questions go. Ask yourself these and other questions as you analyze how people converse. Observe and notice.

In the past, characters were allowed to get away with giving long, drawn out speeches in dialog, in ways that, to the modern reader, at least, can come across as if the character were standing at a podium, even when there is some back-and-forth. Such passages often read as if all the speakers came prepared with scripts (or at the very least prompters behind the curtains!), ready and able to throw about the most flowery "spontaneous" bits of idle conversation imaginable.

For example, consider this passage from Jane Austen's *Pride and Prejudice*:

"Design! Nonsense, how can you talk so! But it is very likely that he *may* fall in love with one of them, and therefore you must visit him as soon as he comes."

"I see no occasion for that. You and the girls may go, or you may send them by themselves, which perhaps will be still better, for as you are as handsome as any of them, Mr. Bingley may like you the best of the party."

"My dear, you flatter me. I certainly *have* had my share of beauty, but I do not pretend to be anything extraordinary now. When a woman has five grown-up daughters, she ought to give over thinking of her own beauty."

"In such cases, a woman has not often much beauty to think of."

"But, my dear, you must indeed go and see Mr. Bingley when he comes into the neighbourhood."

"It is more than I engage for, I assure you."

"But consider your daughters. Only think what an establishment it would be for one of them. Sir William and Lady Lucas are determined to go, merely on that account, for in general, you know, they visit no newcomers. Indeed you must go, for it will be impossible for *us* to visit him if you do not."

"You are over-scrupulous, surely. I dare say Mr. Bingley will be very glad to see you; and I will send a few lines by you to assure him of my hearty consent to his marrying whichever he chooses of the girls; though I must throw in a good word for my little Lizzy."

"I desire you will do no such thing. Lizzy is not a bit better than the others; and I am sure she is not half so handsome as Jane, nor half so good-humoured as Lydia. But you are always giving *her* the preference."

"They have none of them much to recommend them," replied he; "they are all silly and ignorant like other girls; but Lizzy has something more of quickness than her sisters."

"Mr. Bennet, how *can* you abuse your own children in such a way? You take delight in vexing me. You have no compassion for my poor nerves."

"You mistake me, my dear. I have a high respect for your nerves. They are my old friends. I have heard you mention them with consideration these last twenty years at least."

From *Pride and Prejudice*, Chapter 1

Perhaps those in the same social class indeed made idle conversation with such flair and rhythm, but I dare the modern author to try to get away with *that* kind of dialog!

Another indulgence permitted authors of the past was the near-monolog. These, too, read as if the character is standing at a podium, reading a prepared speech on their life's philosophy. Unless the passage *is* a character standing on a podium giving such a speech, in modern fiction these indulgences are best avoided.

As is pointed out in a later section on style, readers sometimes permit these transgressions, but only because they forgive great authors great sins. What Jack London had coming out of the mouth of Martin Eden so many years ago simply would not flow from the mouths of today's characters:

> "Why didn't you dare it before?" he asked harshly. "When I hadn't a job? When I was starving? When I was just as I am now, as a man, as an artist, the same Martin Eden? That's the question I've been propounding to myself for many a day—not concerning you merely, but concerning everybody. You see I have not changed, though my sudden apparent appreciation in value compels me constantly to reassure myself on that point. I've got the same flesh on my bones, the same ten fingers and toes. I am the same. I have not developed any new strength nor virtue. My brain is the same old brain. I haven't made even one new generalization on literature or philosophy. I am personally of the same value that I was when nobody wanted me. And what is puzzling me is why they want me now. Surely they don't want me for myself, for myself is the same old self they did not want. Then they must want me for something else, for something that is outside of me, for something that is not I! Shall I tell you what that something is? It is for the recognition I have received. That recognition is not I. It resides in the minds of others. Then again for the money I have earned and am earning. But that money is not I. It resides in banks and in the pockets of Tom, Dick, and Harry. And is it for that, for the recognition and the money, that you now want me?"
>
> "You are breaking my heart," she sobbed. "You know I love you, that I am here because I love you."
>
> "I am afraid you don't see my point," he said gently. "What I mean is: if you love me, how does it happen that you love me now so much more than you did when your love was weak enough to deny me?"

From *Martin Eden*, Chapter 45

Of course she doesn't see his point! Very few listeners could have caught *everything* he had to say, so quickly— his little impromptu outburst carries on for about a printed page! Perhaps Martin ought to have handed her his cue cards, so she could take time to reflect upon what he'd just said! One can imagine how many times Eden must have worked through this speech in his brain before it made its way past his eager lips.

Now that you have taken a look (and a listen!) at how others speak (and how other authors convey that speech), it is time to move to yourself and your own patterns. You know what you *mean* when you utter something, so no one is better qualified to analyze your speech patterns. Does what you mean come out *the way* you mean it? Do the people listening to you seem to get your point? When you begin forming your next sentence in a conversation in which you are involved, are you listening to the person speaking to you, or do you reply before fully processing what they have said? Do others tend to interrupt you in mid-thought, and do you tend to interrupt them? Do you get flustered when speaking with someone who does not seem to understand what you are saying? What do you do as a result: wave your hands, fold your arms, eat your bile?

To write effective dialog, you will have to examine these issues. It is not important that you may discover that you tend to interrupt people, or that you never quite seem able to get your point across to others when speaking—this is not a class in effective public speaking or active listening. What is important is that you take note of these things and try to capture them in the dialog of your characters when you write dialog in your fiction. All of the quirks, emotional reactions, misunderstandings, rude guffaws, half-completed thoughts, changes of topic, and waved arms amount to something, and if you learn to translate these things into your written dialog, you will be well on your way to writing realistic dialog.

DRAMA WITH LOUDER BEATS

Theatrical pieces are heavily dialog-oriented. Although theatrical prose will not be discussed in depth here, there is a device in modern theatre, the parenthetical beat, that will be examined. The (beat) allows the playwright to indicate his intention to the player that the character speaking undergoes some change of direction, emotion, intent, or motive that ought to be clearly indicated by the player.

The playwright leaves just what that change in characterization is to the actors and director to decide, by context. Actors and directors are not necessarily fond of the *wryly*, that is, a parenthetical indication of how the playwright feels the actor should say something. (Jackson said, begrudgingly.)

In the following scene from *Empty Rooms*, for instance, notice the use of beats to indicate some change of character mood (that the audience should somehow be able to notice in the acting):

> **JACKIE**. She's gone forever now. (Beat.) I didn't lie. I really can't keep up with your poetry. It's beyond me, and I admit it.
>
> **CHRIS**. But that line about Georges Beaufort—that was beautiful. You may as well have told her you know Dylan Thomas. Beaufort's been dead for years.
>
> **JACKIE**. (Beat.) He's not dead. (Pause.) Just drunk. (Longer pause.) I do know him. He's my uncle on my mother's side.

Excerpt from *Empty Rooms* (Act I, Scene 3)

The conversation above, written as prose, might read:

> "She's gone *forever* now," Jack signed. She then looked at Chris, realizing that he'd probably heard enough of her moaning about the whole matter. He wanted to talk about Georges. "I didn't lie," she insisted. "I really *can't* keep up with your poetry. It's beyond me," she sighed, "and I admit it."
>
> "But that line about Georges Beaufort—that was beautiful," Chris returned. He knew it was a lie, unless she didn't know Beaufort was dead. "You may as well have told her you know Dylan Tomas. Beaufort's been dead for years."
>
> What would it take to get Chris to snap out of his naïve bubble? She was starting to get mad. "He's not dead." She paced a bit. "Just drunk." After it seemed that Chris got the idea, she explained, "I do know him. He's my uncle on my mother's side."

Excerpt from *Empty Rooms*, recast as prose

In the theatrical presentation, beats require competent dramatic interpretation. Different directors will interpret the beats differently, or even ignore the playwright's tap on the shoulder. In fiction, however, the author can bang the beat loudly, as in the recast version.

In fiction, what I am here calling the "loud beat" in dialog is the piece of exposition between phrases—sometimes right in the middle of an utterance—that explains what is going on inside the speaker that drives the pendulum of the dialog to suddenly swing.

How loudly any given beat can be drummed is a matter that answers to the story, the characters, and the effect the author wishes to achieve. Loudly gonged beats in prose can sometimes read awkwardly, as in the following example:

"I love you, with all my life," he said. "I'd give anything for you." As he was reaching into his pocket to find the engagement ring he'd spent six months' salary to buy, he saw something that reminded him what she did to him. His blood started to boil. He stood, eyes flaming with hatred, and yelled, "Get the hell out of here before I call the cops!"

Perhaps too *loud* a beat

Such sudden turns can occur in dialog that ends up not reading as if one is reading a conversation overheard in an asylum for the criminally insane, to be sure, but care should be taken to keep such beats to the flow of the story. Perhaps they require a bit more development; even a few paragraphs might be better.

55

HE SAID, SHE SAID (SAID HE, SAID SHE)

"I fear," said she, "your sons have gone astray.

My daughters left me while I slept."

"Yes'm," the Badger said: "it's as you say.

"They should be better kept."

—Lewis Carroll, "The Three Badgers"

This section is not about the gender of protagonists in fiction, but rather, about what is possibly the most often discussed verb in any book on writing fiction: *to say*. Some books go so far as to list many alternatives to forms of the verb, such as: *declare, pronounce, mumble, utter,* and *whisper*. Such lists of words are supposed to provide the author with alternatives to that lovely Anglo-Saxon monosyllable, just in case the author should ever find himself lacking a suitable verb, one might suppose. Others declare that modern fiction should be direct, and that the various forms of *to say* do the best job of achieving this end.

Were I to be asked for a pronouncement on the matter, I would mumble under my breath, uttering my opinion at barely a whisper, "Use whatever word that works best under the particular circumstances of each utterance." It is (or should be, anyway) the narrative itself that tells us what works best in any particular situation, not some proscriptive proclamation.

Writers are still permitted to have a personal style, and were we all to have our characters *saying* this and *saying* that, the word would serve about as much purpose as a full stop at the end of a sentence, and if all it does is do that, why bother attributing speech in the first place? Quotation marks and other punctuation would be enough in a world populated exclusively by *saids*.

So, do you want a list, then? In the real world we all inhabit, people *yell*, they *holler*, they *notice out loud*, they *muse*, they *exclaim*, they *wonder*, they *demand*, and the list goes on. Fiction is *not* the real world, but to some degree captures reality in the written word. How could all of the ways that people get words out of their mouths and to the ears of others be reduced to *one* verb?

Let us take a look at how a master did it. by considering this passage of dialog from *Martin Eden*, taking particular note of how London makes use of the pauses between quotations to carry the dialog along. London does not just have two people speaking in the following passage, but has them *interacting* as living, breathing human beings:

"When did you love me?" she whispered.

"From the first, the very first, the first moment I laid eye on you. I was mad for love of you then, and in all the time that has passed since then I have only grown the madder. I am maddest, now, dear. I am almost a lunatic, my head is so turned with joy."

"I am glad I am a woman, Martin—dear," she said, after a long sigh.

He crushed her in his arms again and again, and then asked:—

"And you? When did you first know?"

"Oh, I knew it all the time, almost, from the first."

"And I have been as blind as a bat!" he cried, a ring of vexation in his voice. "I never dreamed it until just how, when I—when I kissed you."

"I didn't mean that." She drew herself partly away and looked at him. "I meant I knew you loved almost from the first."

"And you?" he demanded.

"It came to me suddenly." She was speaking very slowly, her eyes warm and fluttery and melting, a soft flush on her cheeks that did not go away. "I never knew until just now when—you put your arms around me. And I never expected to marry you, Martin, not until just now. How did you make me love you?"

"I don't know," he laughed, "unless just by loving you, for I loved you hard enough to melt the heart of a stone, much less the heart of the living, breathing woman you are."

"This is so different from what I thought love would be," she announced irrelevantly.

"What did you think it would be like?"

"I didn't think it would be like this." She was looking into his eyes at the moment, but her own dropped as she continued, "You see, I didn't know what this was like."

From *Martin Eden*, Chapter 21

Yes, despite the already cited monolog from a later chapter of *Martin Eden*, London was a master of dialog. It's clear from the above excerpt that he knew how people *really* talk, and perhaps it is because this is so clear that the monologs get a nod when they leak into the work.

Ultimately, after you have given it its due consideration, what you have people saying in your fiction, and how you have your narrators attributing their words rests squarely with you as the writer. Do try to be bold, or timid, if the story calls for it as you see the story, and say it well, and your readers will forgive the occasional remark, reply, retort, and utterance.

Character Mechanics

"I shouldn't know you again if we *did* meet," Humpty Dumpty replied in a discontented tone, giving her one of his fingers to shake: "you're so exactly like other people."

"The face is what one goes by, generally," Alice remarked in a thoughtful tone.

"That's just what I complain of," said Humpty Dumpty. "Your face is the same as everybody has—the two eyes, so—" (marking their places in the air with his thumb) "nose in the middle, mouth under. It's always the same. Now if you had the two eyes on the same side of the nose, for instance—or the mouth at the top—that would be *some* help."

—Lewis Carroll, *Through the Looking-Glass*

Character in fiction is partly aesthetic and partly mechanical, and so the present chapter shall only deal with the mechanical and leave the aesthetic considerations for later in this book.

NAMES

"It's a stupid name enough!" Humpty Dumpty interrupted impatiently. "What does it mean?"

"*Must* a name mean something?" Alice asked doubtfully.

"Of course it must," Humpty Dumpty said with a short laugh: "*my* name means the shape I am—and a good handsome shape it is, too. With a name like yours, you might be any shape, almost."

—Lewis Carroll, *Through the Looking-Glass*

Every character in fiction has a name, except when he or she doesn't. I don't say this to be flippant, since in the novel *Abadoun*, two key characters travel through the entire novel without names, and moreover, the protagonist of Knut Hamsun's *Hunger* also is never named.

Most characters, however, especially most protagonists, have names, and those names, being part of the fiction, play a role in the fiction itself. To select those names at random or without care is to throw away an opportunity to add something to the narrative.

In the real world, parents often name their children with names that mean something they want their children to *become*. In fiction, the author has the special privilege of being able to name characters something they *already are*.

As will be mentioned later in the chapter on symbols and allusion, names can also be used to invoke references to other literature. For instance, in *The Succubus Sea*, the protagonist's love interest is named Salomeh, and she happens to be a dancer.

Beyond the meaning of names, there is the sound of names. Any name rhyming with *said* will, if the name of a character who speaks a lot, inevitably come out sounding odd, as in *Ted said* or *Jed said*. Of course, just as artists who cannot draw hands very well often have the people in their drawings put their hands in their pockets or behind their backs, it is entirely possible to simply avoid the use of the verb said whenever *Ned* speaks.

Although there are a lot of Johns in the English speaking world, too many Johns or Marys or Janes in the same story will confuse the reader (and possibly confuse you, the author). Fortunately, in the fictional world, everyone in a novel can have a unique first name.

Another consideration when naming characters is to avoid using the names of people you know. First names may be fine (there are, as has already been discussed, many Johns in this world), but to use the entire name of a living person might be seen as an invasion, even if the character is not based on his namesake. This applies also to fictional characters, since there can only be one Hannibal Lector (one would hope).

HISTORIES

Characters in fiction have a past. If you don't know the histories of your main characters, it may result in historical oddities cropping up. For instance, if your American protagonist of your story was ten-years-old during the Korean war, and was also a Vietnam veteran, then he was likely in his early twenties while in Vietnam. Could he have received a copy of Dylan Thomas' poetry collection *Deaths and Entrances* for his tenth birthday? How old (roughly) was he in the late nineties? To answer that question, you have to know some real world history as well as the character's fabricated history.

How much history must you concoct for your characters? At the very least you should know their age, their era, and thereby their place alongside major world events. Knowing their age, you also must know the cultural influences they likely experienced, and that will take some research if you were not part of that era or culture. All the details of their histories need not come out in the fiction, but if you are not careful, the inconsistencies *will*.

MOTIVES

Real people do things for reasons, even if they are unaware of those reasons. Need-driven motive serves as the basis of what is now called Maslow's hierarchy of needs.[1] At a most basic level, human beings are driven by their need to breathe, eat and drink, sleep, have sex, and to urinate and defecate. Once these physiological needs have been met, humans seek to be safe in their ability to provide for their families, protect their property and resources, and to protect their bodies. This taken care of, they seek

---

[1]   Abraham Maslow, "A Theory of Human Motivation," *Psychological Review*, Vol. 50, pp. 370-396, 1943.

friendship and family bonds, and sexual intimacy. If they can achieve these things, they then seek self-esteem and the esteem of others.

Understanding human motivation is critical to driving fiction. If you have a character walk into a room, and don't know *why* that character is entering the room, you are only halfway there. What if another character should ask, "What are you doing here?" and you don't have a plausible answer to come out of the first character's mouth? Do you think your characters are going to not ask questions like that? If it's two o'clock in the morning while you're writing the passage, they very well may.

Do these motives have to come out in the narrative? Not necessarily, but consider the difference between: "He walked into the kitchen to make a sandwich" and "he walked into the kitchen to make sure the back door was locked." Is there much difference between the two sentences? In one case, the motive is to satisfy the physiological need to eat, and in the other, the motive is to affirm   security. Saying simply "he walked into the kitchen" conveys no attempt at satisfaction of motive.

If your characters are always going about without motive or purpose, however, they may start to read like balls in a billiard game: knocked about by chance.

The motives behind a character's actions also allow you, as the author, some guidelines about what to discuss in the narrative, and how to present it.

For instance, if a woman returning home from an overly long visit with a neighbor wishes to please her husband by making some bread with honey for him (without his finding out that she had to borrow some), her motive for hurrying becomes clearer to the reader:

"I—"

"Take the clothes, dear child, so you do not insult me with your rejection of my good things. They were not too good for me when my mother offered them to me. Boukhara and Samarqand they're not, but they're mine to give, and mine to squander as I will. We agreed not to play *ta'arof*, Fatimeh."

Her smile extended widely and you could not refuse her supplication; you stretched out your hand and took the gifts that she offered. Finally, she had no more clothes to give and it was time to return home before Bahram awoke.

As you hurried home, you passed an intersection where normally only beasts of burden would pass. A quick glance over your shoulder yielded a view of a car. You had wanted your husband in Shiraz to have a car just like this. Or, if not like this man's car, perhaps larger. You had not seen many cars come to Abadoun, and admitted to yourself that you really had no idea how large they could be, but your dreams of life in Shiraz had never included donkeys and horses—just cars of one kind or another.

Soon the car turned at the intersection and was on its way. You were not much later again in front of your own home with Bahram's honey and Mrs. Ghassemi's precious things. You opened the door and your question was soon answered. Bahram was awake.

"I see you've come back at last," he said, his voice still strange to your ears and nothing like you had imagined the Shirazi accent would be. He did not speak Kurdish at all, and you were obliged to struggle with what Persian you had been taught during Shah's time just to understand his words.

"Yes, my husband," you replied. If you reached the kitchen quickly enough, you reasoned, he would not suspect that you had been out looking for honey for his bread.

"For a Husband from Shiraz"

We can see why she *hurried* home, rather than walked slowly. She did not wish for him to find out that she had to borrow food. Even such mundane motives as avoiding having a husband know that one had to borrow something from a neighbor (so as not to hurt his pride) are human motives, and fiction is about human beings, and human beings often rush, hurry, and stress themselves out over the mundane.

Knowing Fatimeh's motive about the honey, then, and her wish to not have her husband know she had borrowed food, the following passage takes on deeper meaning:

"I remembered that I had some baby clothes to pick up from Mrs. Ghassemi, and that she had eggs for us. She says you should take more eggs with your meals to build your strength, so you can get out and about in the mountain air."

You were almost at the kitchen door when he said, "Her sons' baby things, then?"

You didn't want to reply, but felt obliged by the prying tone of his voice. "Girl things for the daughters she never had. She was quite insistent," you almost apologized to him. "I told her it was useless, since I'm carrying a son, but—"

"For a Husband from Shiraz"

Fatimeh admits to the eggs and the baby clothes, and "almost apologizes" over the clothes. Why not mention the honey? Knowing her motive, the reader can assume that the eggs were part of Fatimeh's regular routine, and she probably had a barter arrangement for them, whereas the honey was a loan. A mountain out of a molehill? In serious fiction, short fiction especially, there are (or should be) no molehills when it comes back to motive, for it is often the fuel for conflict.

CONFLICT

Fiction is often moved from beginning, to middle, to ending by some form of conflict. The source of the conflict can be from within the protagonist, from other characters, or from the environment. These three forms of conflict are often referred to as *Man against Himself, Man against Man*, and *Man against Nature*. As I understand conflict in serious fiction, however, it all amounts to *Man against Himself*, since when a human being faces nature or another human being, he is ultimately facing himself, not some external force. As will be discussed in a later chapter, character movement is important to the overall effectiveness of a piece. The primary impetus for character movement is some form of conflict.

If a piece begins in its first paragraph with a woman standing at the edge of the ocean about to jump in to her death, the conflict is clear: she finds a way out of that state of mind, or she dies. Conflict need not be so dramatic, certainly, but it must exist at some level if the story is to move the protagonist in some genuine and meaningful direction.

Conflict can be conveyed by any of the various means already discussed: scene-setting, information filtered through a POV, the passage of time, and dialog.

In a first person narrative, conflict can be created by having the character misinterpret the intentions of the other characters in the story. Even the passage of time can be used to effectively create conflict: something that would not be stressful to a character given a month to complete can become a major challenge if that same character is given only two days to do the job. Finally, since so much of human crisis is the result of people opening their mouths and spouting off, dialog (both internal and external) can both create and aggravate conflict of just about any kind.

Consider how this excerpt from the story "Two Brothers" uses internal and external dialog to show the constant state of conflict between the two brothers:

> Sometimes Reza would invite Mahmoud over to his apartment for holidays that Mahmoud had never heard of in Urmieh. Thanksgiving. What was this? To whom were they to give thanks? The thought of thanking anyone for sending him here without consulting his academic credentials to drive a taxi—he was a teacher! He'd taught at the college in Urmieh for ten years before the Revolution. Would he thank the immigration officer on this Thanksgiving?
>
> "You should consider yourself damned lucky to be coming here!" the officer had said. "We saved your life, and now you owe it to us to try your hardest to fit in." Was this what the turkey on his brother's table was for? In Urmieh, they never sat at a table to eat. Was the turkey the immigration officer in effigy, there to be carved up?
>
> "*Pedar-sukhteh!*" he cursed at his brother. Reza's latest girlfriend, a saleswoman from Quebec, sat at the other side of the table as Reza cut up the turkey for Mahmoud. "What about last *Sizdah beh Dar*, Dadash? I invited you to my place for that...."
>
> "What nonsense!" Reza returned as he served the white meat to his younger brother. "We are here now, Mahmoud. We don't have that here. Here, New Year is January."

"New Year's," Cecile corrected Reza's English.

"What?"

"We say 'New Year's,' as in 'New Year's Day.' You said 'New Year.'"

Reza nodded his head at his girlfriend and smiled. "You see, Mahmoud? The Canadians know how important it is to speak proper English. Thank you, Cecile."

Mahmoud held in his anger. Finally, he turned to Cecile and asked, "Is true? When I teached in Iran, I teached that the proud persons of Quebec fight for cultural independency. The FLQ—"

"Two Brothers"

Mahmoud recalls the words spoken to him by the immigration officer, and this primes him to swear at his brother. (*Pedar-sukhteh* is a Farsi insult literally translated to mean, "[Your] father burned!") Reza then chastises his brother, and Cecile corrects her boyfriend's English usage, further aggravating the situation. Everyone gets involved in the mix, and the tension level in the room grows higher.

Conflict need not be Earth-shattering for it to be significant to the movement of a piece. Nobody's life need be on the line for the stakes to be high enough to merit calling something a conflict. Conflict can be shown in "little" ways:

"If you want to be a novelist, you'd have to get some discipline, and you just don't have it," Ken added, still reading his paper. A trail of smoke from his cigarette poured up, over the edge of the sports section. "Take Hemingway. I read somewhere that he sat at his typewriter every day until he had five thousand words behind him. Every day. No exceptions."

Upon hearing this again, for the third time in a week, Mark wanted to repeat out loud another mantra Ken had used on him almost weekly: *Believe none of what you hear, very little of what you read, and only half of what you see.* Instead, he finally said what was on his mind. "I've written plenty of stories." He held up the science fiction piece he was working on as tangible evidence.

"That's a pamphlet," Ken commented over the top of the paper. "Five thousand words a day," he repeated himself. "Every day. Discipline."

"It Ain't Never Gonna Happen"

Nobody loses a limb over the conflict that exists between Mark and Ken, but the *tension* is clear. Mark is also at odds with Tim, his brother-in-law, who has been taking advantage of the family situation, and this leads to punches being thrown when Tim's dog urinates on Mark's handwritten novel manuscript:

> Beside his bed sat a pile of yellow stained papers, strewn about. His heart pounded as he slowly approached his novel. Pools of urine and ink smears lay where once was his novel, his discipline.
>
> "*Who* opened my door?" he screamed so loudly he could feel his tonsils push into his ears. When he turned around, the first face he saw was Tim's.
>
> "I guess you have your first major critic," Tim barely had time to say before Mark had his hands around his neck.
>
> When he awoke the next day, under an icepack, Mark could not remember what had happened during the brawl from the moment he'd grabbed Tim. His mother was leaning over him, shifting the pack over his eye, sighing.
>
> "Did I at least take one of his teeth out?" he managed to ask.

"It Ain't Never Gonna Happen"

Finally, Mark is brought into conflict with his own ego and need for recognition when he must decide whether or not to tell his stepfather that the reason he has not produced the novel he claimed he could is that Tim's dog destroyed it.

> He looked up at his mother with his good eye. She was visibly afraid of what Ken's reaction would be if he gave up the fact that Tim and Jane had kept their dog at the house. He wouldn't do that to his mother.
>
> The final week of the two months passed slowly with Mark staying in his room, in bed, recovering from being hit in the eye. The swelling was almost completely down by the time Ken came back from the rigs.
>
> After a big dinner, Ken walked up to Mark's bedroom door, knocked, and looked in. "So how's my little novelist doing?" he asked, clearly amused with himself. "Where's the novel you said you were going to write?"

From the darkness, with a sheet pulled over his face like a newspaper, Mark replied, "I didn't write one. I guess I lack *discipline*. It ain't ever gonna happen."

"It Ain't Never Gonna Happen"

None of these "little" aggravations in Mark's life is too severe, but they do move the story from one point to the next, and ultimately result in Mark's selfless act of obedience to his mother's wishes at the end of the story. Mark is moved from a selfish desire to prove himself to his stepfather to a selfless desire to protect his mother's interests, and this through the various conflicts of the narrative. As already discussed in the previous section on motives, life is full of mundane disasters.

FUNCTIONAL AND MINOR CHARACTERS

What I am here calling functional characters are those characters who find their way into a piece to serve some function of the story. These characters provide the author with a means of telling something, connecting two or more dots, or motivating another character to take some action. Are such characters legitimate in serious fiction? I believe they are, and from time to time employ the functional character on as as-needed basis.

For instance, in *The Succubus Sea*, the protagonist needs a way to get into Iran with his girlfriend. Since the laws and social customs of such a tightly Islamic country would not permit him to simply fly to Iran with a girlfriend (and still be able to sleep in her room), Drake obtains forged marriage papers.

Up to that point in the novel, there are no characters who could provide him with such papers, and so, in passing, a functional character appears and disappears to suit this purpose:

> Drake thought about it. "We're only living together, but I can get some paperwork done up that makes it look like we're married so that we can enter Iran together. One of my students earns a little extra college money as a forger. Government bureaucrats are nothing, if not impressed by pretty paperwork. That and a few bribes will get us through."

From *The Succubus Sea*, Chapter 13

> Having marriage papers forged proved simple and inexpensive enough, since James Defoe, one of Drake's better senior students, had five originals in his sample collection to choose from, and was therefore able to pick one from a state that required very little effort and expense to forge. After making a few international long distance calls and participating in some ritual bribery to get over the obvious questions, Drake and Salomeh had visas, she as a German and he as an American. Since his record was clear, and since the office had no trouble finding his Iranian birth records, he had very little difficulty.

From *The Succubus Sea*, Chapter 14

This form of functional character is a character who is talked about by others, and possibly even plays a key role in the story, but never actually makes a full-fledged appearance in the fiction.

Such a character also figures in "Jimmy the Fin":

> They're over there chatting it up, she's all smiles, giggles, and grins, kissing him on the cheek, thanking him I guess. Finally, he comes back to me and asks me if I have any money.
>
> "I'd have paid for the bottle rather than see you lose your fiver to Joe if I had any money, Jimmy, you know that," I says. "I'd have floated you the deuce."
>
> He just gives me a look like I ain't never seen from him before, and shrugs at me.
>
> Nicest guy I ever knew, Jimmy the Fin. Lucky in cards, lucky with women, lucky all around. But he lost his fiver and now here we were, with no soda left in our bottles, and damn it was hot, and he

had nothing in his pockets to take Missy Leduc dancing and eating with.

"Georgie," he says.

Now, the only man ever borrow money from Georgie is looking to get his kneecaps broken, and I tell Jimmy this. He knows it already, but Jimmy, he ain't thinking straight, and so we head for Georgie's place. Five minutes later, he's walking out of the place, flipping them sweet bills like they were his. But I know they ain't his. They are Georgie's bills, not Jimmy's, and if Georgie don't get them back, Jimmy won't be dancing with no woman come the end of the week. But Jimmy was in love, and he was my friend, and friends don't go making no trouble and noise when their friends are in love, so I keep my trap shut.

So Jimmy goes walking down the road, tells me to find something to do while he takes Missy Leduc eating and dancing, and I do like he says and find things to do. It wasn't two days later that I come across Jimmy, all busted and broken.

"Jimmy the Fin"

When is a minor character just a functional character? If the character actually makes an appearance, has a few things to say, and gets more involved than we've seen here, that character may indeed be a minor, rather than functional character. The distinction between the two kinds of small players is really not all that important.

Probably more important is when *major* characters are, when all is said and done, used primarily as functional characters. It is my feeling that such characters are best avoided. If a character takes on a larger role than you anticipated he or she would, perhaps it is time to flesh that character out a bit and consider digging a little deeper into characterization, in order to avoid having major players in your narrative who come across as cardboard cutouts or imitations of human beings.

Sex, Sexuality, and Eroticism

Of the delights of this world man cares most for sexual intercourse, yet he has left it out of his heaven.

—Mark Twain

Perhaps, as Twain observed, sex is left out of heaven, but it is not always left out of serious fiction. Serious fiction is ultimately about and for real human beings, and except for those born by means of artificial insemination, every real human being alive today (or who has ever been alive) is the result of sexual intercourse.

Because much of my fiction is about adult relationships, much of it has sexual and erotic overtones. In some cases, such as in the short story "Washed Up," the sex is matter-of-fact. In other stories, such as "Touched to the Bone," the act of two fictional characters having sex is intermingled with heavy metaphysical symbolism.

THE NAKED TRUTH ABOUT SEX IN FICTION

Sometimes in my dreams there are women....When such dreams happen, immediately I remember, "I am a monk." ... It is very important to analyze "What is the real benefit of sexual desire?" The appearance of a beautiful face or a beautiful body—as many scriptures describe—no matter how beautiful, they essentially decompose into a skeleton. When we penetrate to its human flesh and bones, there is no beauty, is there?

—The Dalai Lama

The human body is a masterpiece of architecture. When one studies visual art, one typically undergoes a detailed study of the human body. One learns that the ridge under the human nose that connects to the upper lip is called the *philtrum* and that, on a "perfectly proportioned" adult face, the corner of the lips pretty much line up to the center of the pupils. While human faces differ, and many people's faces do not match up exactly to what the artist studies as "perfect" proportions, when a trained portrait artist looks at a face, he *instinctively* knows how a given face differs from the so-called ideal.

A large part of learning to draw the human form correctly as an artist is learning how to stare at a naked human body and render it onto paper. This training, in addition to allowing the artist to build hand-eye coordination, serves another purpose: it teaches the artist to be at ease while watching a nude model. Over time, the "appearance of a beautiful face or a beautiful body ... no matter how beautiful" essentially becomes a nearly automatic and emotionless process of decomposing "into a skeleton," and in this fashion, the Dalai Lama's words in this section's epigram show a certain appropriateness.

Whereas visual artists can spend many years practicing drawing the human form before they even begin to do even a half-decent job of capturing its essence well in their art, authors of fiction often fumble about in the dark, struggling with such matters as basic anatomy and years of psychosocial prudery about the various mechanics of the sexual act. Unlike visual artists, who can attend classes just on figure drawing, authors cannot spend years observing other human beings doing what human beings do so well and so often.

Ask ten different authors to describe a naked man, and you are likely to get ten different results. Some will call the male sexual genitalia a *penis*, some will call it a *cock*, others will call it the *male member*, and some might even call it a *dick* or a *prick*. The female genitalia, likewise, may be called any number of things by various authors: a *vagina*, a *pussy*, a *crotch*, a *cunt*, a *twat*, or even a *snatch*. Each of these phrases has a time and a place in fiction, and each carries with it any number of connotations and denotations of which the author must be carefully aware. What an awkward toolbox the author of serious fiction is presented with should he wish to describe two people having sex!

Even the idiomatic expression "to have sex" has many different forms, each with its own baggage. Two people may *have sex, make love, copulate, consummate their love, screw, fuck,* or, should the mood overtake them, *make the two-backed beast.* (Who does the *sleeping* when two people *sleep together*?)

Until you are comfortable with the human body and the fictionalization of sex, you may be tempted to do what amateur artists have been doing with hands and feet on human figure drawing for centuries. Artists who cannot draw hands well simply have their figures put their hands in their pockets or behind their backs (or behind a conveniently placed large object). By skipping such descriptions altogether, you may create the impression that you have strategically left the details for the reader to supply with his imagination, and indeed, some readers may even comment that the sex in your fiction is "tastefully done." Tastefully done sex scenes often simply means those sex scenes that are hidden behind the veil of never really having been written at all.

If you wish to learn how to write smooth sexual passages in your fiction, however, you are going to have to practice your craft until you can write such passages to your own satisfaction as an artist. Some of your practice will inevitably come across reading like pornography, but eventually, if you make an effort to hone your skills, you may be able to write what others give the pseudo-honorable label of *erotica*. If you learn to do it well enough, it will simply be called *fiction*; which is to say that well-written sex in serious fiction does not call attention to itself with any particular special label, it simply flows naturally as part of the greater narrative.

IT ALL STARTS WITH A SIMPLE KISS

In fiction, as in life, kissing can have either sexual or non-sexual implications. Although I am not absolutely certain, I would almost be willing to wager that many adults can think back to their first *passionate* kiss, much in the same way most would be able to remember the loss of their virginity, whereas most would not be able to tell you the first time they received a non-sexual kiss.

Since kissing plays such an important role in both sexual arousal and passionate intimacy, it stands to reason that authors ought to learn how to be comfortable writing their kisses.

One fictional kiss that has resulted in many comments from my readers occurs between Cyrus Drake and Salomeh Arashpour in the novel *The Succubus Sea*:

"You succeeded. Anything else?"

"Well," she said, blowing a smoke ring as she walked towards him, "perhaps I had something more meaningful in mind than just that."

"Oh?"

"I saw the way you looked at me at the funeral," she said.

"And?"

She was now very close to him and he could smell her. He knew he shouldn't be standing so close to the Arashpours' granddaughter, in a dark attic, with the door open, with everyone downstairs and able to come upstairs at any minute, but something inside him, the new heat, didn't care.

Her arm slid around him, pulling him in. She was shorter than he was, but like the dancer, stood on point and kissed him on his lower lip, then bit it. Drake let his lip get bitten. The older, wiser parts of him wanted him to turn his head, but he didn't want to be older and wiser. The touch of her young breasts against his chest, her smell, the taste of her—he bit back and was lost to her tow.

Like the *first* first kiss, heat and shivers shot in the hair on the back of his neck as she searched her mouth with his. It took some of his pain away. Pain. It had only felt like emptiness before. Now he knew it had been pain. He let his hand, still with a lit cigarette burning between his fingers, around her waist and he pulled her closer, higher, so their kiss was deeper. The kiss was not just her kiss, it was their kiss, whatever that meant in the here and now. It was neither hers nor his alone.

His hand slowly caressed her waist, but before he allowed to it come around to the front of her, reason pulled him back, and he just let the kiss continue without such nonsense. He didn't want her lips to leave his, the smoke of her last almost Eastern tea-house opium drag was pouring from both their nostrils. It had to end, but he did not want be the one to end it, so he let it continue. Not let *her* continue, since it was a beast unto itself and it had to be allowed to tire itself out in its cage, but let the new heat continue on its very own.

From *The Succubus Sea*, Chapter 5

The impact of this kiss upon Cyrus Drake is in stark contrast to a kiss between him and Valery Rockford earlier in the novel:

Her climax was its usual explosion, taking with it a bit more of his back, and Drake decided to not even bother pushing for his own. As she came, she pulled his face to hers and kissed him deeply, but the depth was hers, the fire was hers, the sounds were hers, and the powerful bucking of the hips were hers; nothing belonged to him.

From *The Succubus Sea*, Chapter 1

Another passionate first kiss occurs in the short story "The Panther" between Eric and Brooke:

"I'm going to shower," she said once they had removed their shoes. Her face seemed to be inviting Eric to join her, but he did not want to make any assumptions, so he walked out onto the balcony while she showered.

It was cold outside. When Brooke came onto the balcony to join Eric, with her shoulder length hair still wet, her teeth started to chatter. Eric took off his overcoat and put it over her bathrobe. Standing behind her, looking into the wet curls of her hair, he felt completely at ease, as he had all day with her.

"I can't remember having ever had such a pleasant day," he said, his hand still on her shoulder.

"Me neither," she said. "I *really* had a wonderful day with you, Eric." She slowly turned around and leaned forward, asking with her movements for a kiss, and Eric responded by kissing her.

It was a warm, comfortable kiss, even though the air was cold around them on the openness of the balcony. Eric slid his arms under the overcoat, under her bathrobe, and around her bare waist, pulling her closer to him. Her hair was still wet, and he could feel drops of cold water running from her down his own cheek.

"Best step inside," he said, stepping backwards through the open balcony door without releasing his grip.

Once inside, Brooke reached back and shut the balcony door without looking. She leaned forward for another kiss.

Their lips met again, this time without the biting chill of the outdoor air to distract them. In a motion, Eric slid her bathrobe off, and with it fell his overcoat. He could feel her undoing the button on his trousers. There was something between them that, now that it had started, would not end until they had both satisfied their curiosity about it. He wanted to remove his shirt, but he did not want to take his lips from hers.

"The Panther"

Unlike the kiss between Drake and Salomeh in *The Succubus Sea*, this kiss leads to Eric and Brooke ending up in bed together:

Finally, he broke off the kiss, quickly slid his shirt over his head, rather than undoing his buttons, and then held her tightly again, standing at the balcony door, and held his now bare chest to her breasts. The kiss started again as if it had never been interrupted.

He kicked his pants aside when they had fallen sufficiently down his legs. Brooke's hands were on his buttocks, sliding under his boxers, along his flesh. What seemed hours later, but was probably only a few minutes, they both pulled their heads back from one another, without moving anything but their necks.

"Oh man," she said. "That was ... amazing." She reached around, between them, and cupped him in her hand. "Oh man," she sighed. She then led him to her bedroom.

"The Panther"

IMPLYING SEX

As has already been mentioned, sometimes an author "hides" the details when two characters have sex. Hiding the details of what transpires, when not simply a device to avoid having to deal with the awkward choices of words such passages sometimes present, allows the story to go on without unnecessary details and can allow the reader his imagination.

The kiss between Eric and Brooke in "The Panther" leads to their having sex. One might be led to believe, from the physical details given up to the point where Brooke leads Eric to her bedroom that the reader is in for an eyeful. Not so in this case:

> "Oh man," she said. "That was ... amazing." She reached around, between them, and cupped him in her hand. "Oh man," she sighed. She then led him to her bedroom.
>
> After they had made love, Eric lay with his head on her shoulder. Brooke was slowly stroking his hair. Her breathing was not yet regular, and lifted and lowered his head rhythmically. He wanted to fall asleep like this.

"The Panther"

Here, the sex is not actually implied; the narrative goes so far as to say that they made love. Sex can be implied without even pointing out that it actually took place. In the version of "The Torchbearer," that was published in the little magazine *Tickled by Thunder*, care had to be taken that the story did not violate that magazine's policy of avoiding explicit prose.

While no sex explicitly occurs or is even mentioned, it is clear that the following passage implies that Anders and Farrah have sex (at the asterisks, to be exact):

> "But we haven't so much as kissed one another," Anders noted aloud. "We can back out of this, if we do it now, and no one will be the wiser."
>
> Farrah looked straight into Anders' eyes, and said, with cold, mathematical determination, "I am *not* going to do that. Even if it means quitting Cambridge. I *would* be the wiser. You would be the wiser. Let's be fools instead, once in our life."
>
> His hands were hot from flushing. "What have I gotten us both into?" he hissed.
>
> "We are both adults, and we both have our eyes open," she replied.

"We haven't even *kissed* for God's sake," he repeated. "We can back out of this...."

It was then that Farrah Donahue leaned forward, pressed her lips to his, and it was then that he returned their first kiss. The moment he began to respond, to return the affection of the embrace, there was no longer any backing out. The torch had been passed and the relay was in its second leg.

* * *

The horns of the morning traffic sounded on the street three floors below the bedroom window of Farrah Donahue's flat, bringing Anders to consciousness. When he saw the auburn mess of Farrah Donahue's hair, splayed over the almost alabaster skin of her face, his half-expectations of seeing no one there were erased. She seemed entirely asleep.

[...]

"It's unethical."

"To blazes with ethics." She kissed the bridge of his nose. "Who cares?"

"I care about ethics."

"The Torchbearer" (*Tickled by Thunder* version)

The fact that Anders and Farrah have sex is critically important to the meaning of the story, since Anders is Farrah's academic committee head at Cambridge, and the ethical implications of this weigh heavily upon Anders' conscience. The details of what they do when they end up in bed, however, are not as important for the purposes of the version of the story that appeared in *Tickled by Thunder*, and it is thus sufficient that Anders wakes up the next morning in Farrah's apartment and she is still asleep. (Apparently, some who "sleep together" actually *do* end up *sleeping* together. So much for silly euphemisms.)

Another story where the storyline relies heavily on the fact that two characters have had sex, but where that sex is only implied (again in the romantic haze of asterisks), is "Paladin":

She smiled, stood, and came over for his plate. He could smell her perfume when she was this close, and wanted to brush the side of his head into her bosom, but did not. "Why haven't you been around long enough?"

"Gypsy blood, I suppose," he said. "I've been on the road my entire adult life. Acting troupes, book signings, on and on. You take what you can get of human affection in circumstances like that, without necessarily forming a lot of bonds."

Salomeh put the dishes in the kitchen and then returned to the table. She placed a chair at the side of the table, so that she was closer to Cohen. "But *could* you love a woman more than you love your work?" she asked.

In the candlelight, Salomeh looked good enough for him to say, "Yes," and his mouth moved the words before he could stop himself. He realized that he did not know her, and was speaking only from being intoxicated by her good looks, her young body, and the glassy stare she was giving him, but the word came out and he did not speak to contradict himself. "I could. It would depend on whether I wanted to be a hero or a villain."

* * *

Another cigarette butt flew in the New York air, still burning, as Cohen leaned over the balcony. He could hear the thing slide open as he tipped back a mouthful from the bottle directly. Drake walked up beside him, held out his hand for the bottle, took a sip, and then lit up a cigarette and handed it to his friend.

"Beautiful city," Cohen said, his words slurring from his mouth.

"It is indeed," Drake replied, lighting another cigarette, this one for himself.

"Saw Klimt at the MOMA today," Cohen tried to say. "Rube *does* have some Klimt in him, I tell you."

[…]

"What's wrong, Benny?" Drake asked.

Cohen gathered up his courage. "Salomeh and I did the wild thing into next week after dinner." The words were out, into the cold air, falling over the balcony like spent cigarette butts. He put out his chin. "Hit me," he said.

Drake tapped the cleft of Cohen Benjamin's chin with his index finger. His hands smelled of fresh turpentine. "She already told me," he said.

Upon hearing this, Cohen pushed his chin into Drake's finger so that it hurt. "Come on, damn it, hit me hard." His cigarette by now was close to the butt and almost burning between his fingers, so he tossed it.

"Why?" Drake asked. He seemed amused with the whole situation.

Not knowing what to say, Cohen leaned over the balcony again and breathed in a deep breath. He grabbed the bottle from Drake and took a long gulp from it. "Well, I guess, if you hit me, then I'll know you're willing to fight like hell for her, and I won't do anything stupid."

Drake put his arm around his friend again and said, "You've already gone and done something stupid, Benny." He lit another smoke, handed it to Cohen. "And there's nothing I can do about that, now, is there?"

"Paladin"

In "Paladin," although the sex is implied, Cohen admits to it to his friend, leaving the reader to figure out what exactly transpired. That Salomeh has been unfaithful and Cohen has betrayed his friend's trust is more important to the story than what exactly happened between the two.

Another instance of implied sex occurs in the short story "Witness to a Murder":

"Are you uncomfortable?" I asked her.

"This *is* quite insane," she admitted.

"Any more insane than when he stood in the pub and let men chat you up while he stood there?" I asked. "Do you feel any more or any less than when that happened right under his dominion?"

She looked at the floor as if ashamed.

I walked from the table and stood before her. "Listen," I assured her, "you needn't treat me as you would a husband. This is about *him* and *his* understanding of love. It's not about me. I can sleep on the floor until he figures it out."

At first, she stared only at my feet. Slowly, she tipped up her head as I stood there near her and looked into my eyes with that same light she had earlier at the Gerard Bar. She reached out her hand onto mine, placed my palm on her right cheek, and then turned to kiss my palm.

* * *

A month later, the phone rang, and it was Michael.

"Do you *know* it?" I asked him.

"I can never have Laura, can I?" he said. His voice was clear rather than full of sadness.

"Is that what you have learned about that kind of love?" I asked. Laura was still asleep beside me, her arm draped over my chest.

"I can love her, with all my heart and soul, but I cannot have her body ever," he said.

"You understand," I replied. "That is Michael's kind of love. Is that the kind of love you will hold your hand over a flame for? Is it?"

I could hear Laura beginning to stir from the full night of making love we had been through. She kissed my cheek.

"Can you *forever* know that her body is another man's, or no man's, and that your love for her can never, ever, go beyond that? Can you *know* that, and live with it? Can you hold your hand over *that*?"

He simply said, "Thank you," and let the phone back on hook.

She ran her hand down my ribcage.

"You have been witness to a murder," I whispered to her.

"Whose murder?" she asked, still playing my ribcage with her fingernails.

"That's not for us to decide," I replied. "If I were to risk a guess, though," I finally added, "I would say the murder of self-deception. I will be finishing my first novel soon."

Laura held either side of my face with her soft hands and looked deeply into my eyes with her painter's stare. "I would die without you," she said. "I would die if you ever left me, Oscar."

"Witness to a Murder"

In this story, that the man who has taken over the woman's husband's role and the woman end up having sex is important to the theme of the story, but the details of what they do in bed are not critical. That Oscar and Michael have exchanged lives, and that Laura walks right into the exchange as if nothing has happened is more important than what is represented by the asterisks.

CAUGHT IN THE ACT

And then there is the explicit sex. The only advice I can give to an author who wishes to write sexually explicit passages in fiction is to avoid diction shifts and faulty parallelism in terms for body parts. If one writes of a *penis* entering a *pussy*, it sounds as ridiculous as a *cock* going into a *vagina*. Street terms, when mixed with Latinate terms, sound ridiculous, except when the street terms are used only in dialog. Unless the diction level calls for them, the Latinate terms for body parts are probably best avoided altogether, in order that one's fiction not read like a high school sex education class. It is entirely possible to write sexually explicit passages without mentioning either party's genitalia at all, of course, and skillfully put "hands in pockets" or behind a large vase.

Consider this passage from *The Succubus Sea*, wherein Drake and Salomeh finally have sex:

When their lips met, Drake's body became its own master. Salomeh wrapped her legs around him, and her toned calves and thighs made his buttocks shake. His tongue touched the top of her mouth. Although his mind remembered that he'd been in a fight, he did not feel any pain. She was pulling at him with her strong legs, trying to get him into her, and he wanted to be in her. The moment came when the tip of his penis touched her, and when it did, she thrust up at him, so that he entered her, just a bit.

He broke the kiss for a moment, to whisper to her, "You are so tight," but he was not sure if the words were intelligible. There was something about her tightness that was new to him, something that he did not understand. She was certainly wet, ready to make love—her whole body told him that. He broke the kiss to speak again, ready to ask a question, but she shushed him and continued to arch up to him so that he would enter her more deeply. *Are you a virgin?* he had wanted to ask, but since she had silenced him with a deep, penetrating kiss as she pulled him into her, the words could only ring in his mind. Soon, even their echo went away, and he allowed his weight to press on her, and he was completely taken in.

His pubic bone pressed against hers. Salomeh slowly raked her fingernails at the small of his back as he used his weight to press her farther up towards the middle of the bed. She bit his lip on one of his thrusts, and this made him thrust more deeply.

Salomeh put her right hand down at their union, feeling around the width of him, gripping him as he thrust, massaging their union with her soft, smooth fingers, as if trying to pull him deeper into herself. Her breasts were crushed against his chest. He knew he could have supported more of his weight on his elbows or hands, but he wanted to put the full force of his body at their loins, so he restrained himself from supporting his own weight.

The sensation of her fingers, down at the junction of him and her, increased his pleasure, but he was not ready to climax. He wanted to enjoy being inside her, and he could tell from the movements of her body and the soft, deep rumble in her that she was completely enjoying having him there.

Since they were chained together by their kiss, he could feel her breathing as if it were his own, and he knew that its pattern was beginning to change. Her grip around the girth of his penis became more desperate, she reached around his buttock and pulled at him, and as she did so, he started to allow himself to drift a bit from his control, and his thrusting became less controlled. He tightened his abdomen so that, as he slipped almost completely out of her and then in again, it would rub firmly against her, making his strokes continual. He grasped at her ass, holding her buttocks firmly, using his whole body's movement for her pleasure.

At first, he thought the deep groan was his own, but he realized it was originating from deep down in her throat, carried up to his throat by the lock of their mouths, and when he felt this, he quickly grasped both her hands with his own, tying his fingers between hers, up above her head, holding her down.

Her eyes opened, with the scream of an approaching climax clear in them, the flash of complete abandon just moments away, and his grip on her hands became tighter. After two more thrusts, he felt her loins begin to squeeze, her eyes became completely lost in a world that was their world, and the moan in his throat that was hers became a muffled roar.

As she came, he continued to thrust into her, and their kiss broke, releasing her groan into the outside world like the demons sprung from Pandora's box. It was at this moment that Drake released deep into her, completely lost in a blinding flash of swirls and novae, but he continued to thrust, since she was still writhing under him. They were slick now, from his wash of semen, but she continued to press up to him. As she slowly came down from her heights and he his, he pressed up, deep into her, still half-hard, and allowed his weight to rest on her. She loosened her hands from his grip, reached down to his buttocks again, and gently pulled him up, even more deeply.

Drake slowly pulled out of her. He felt obligated to say, "If you're not taking the pill, no worries. I made sure of that, years ago."

"*Hin ist hin*," Salomeh replied gently in German.

From *The Succubus Sea*, Chapter 12

As explicit sex goes, that passage leaves only very little to the imagination, and yet manages to avoid Latinate or street terms. The single use of the term *loins* allows for the avoidance of any number of words that would likely not match the diction level of the rest of the passage.

An equally explicit but sufficiently obscured passage occurs in the short story "The Rest of the Wicked":

> One night, she directed me to turn into a dark way. She stood in the boat, undid her bodice, and bid me approach her. I did, and she took my hand and put it on her bare, beating left breast. My hand, though cold to the touch of any mortal who could sleep, grew warm again after thousands of years of never having been so. She took my fingers to her lips and kissed them, and then, with her arms, slowly pulled me to her.
>
> As a gondolier during such times as these were, I knew this was my invitation. She was my sacrifice, and I knew her that night. I tasted her mouth in mine, felt her tongue along my very teeth, felt her legs wrapped around me as we made love. I knew the recesses of her, and knew the fire of her folds on me. Our hearts beat together and as one, our mouths breathed a common breath, as we slid against one another like the waves against the beaches, like the Nile against the shores. No creature on earth was unaware what we were doing, even though none saw us there, in the darkness of that sideway. When it was done, when our pleasure had consumed us both, when we had espied the Disk of Ra himself, she held my head to her breast and let me listen to her beating heart, and for a moment, a taste of a moment, I felt as if–ah, it was a foreigner to me!—I felt as if I was about to taste *sleep*.

"The Rest of the Wicked"

Explicit sexual passages need not be entirely about what is going on physically between two people. The entirety of Chapter 48 of *Janus Incubus*, while a recounting of a casual sexual encounter between Cohen Benjamin and the college student Lilith Pflaum, is actually not so much about the physical act of sex, but about what Cohen is thinking and feeling about his career as an author:

> As Lilith Pflaum straddled Cohen, he with his hands on either side of her waist, almost, but not quite able to imagine touching his index fingers together, she was so slender, Cohen disappeared into

the moment. He slid his hands up her smooth, young back, to her shoulders, and pulled her down from the shoulders as he pushed up. Her kiss was sweet, tasting of lipstick.

She pulled away from the kiss, arching her back, and he took her breasts, pressed them together, and started to taste her nipples. This was what it meant to be an acclaimed author while still in his prime—to have a willing literature graduate on top of him in her dorm, in her bed, and to know that he could catch the next jet, to the next reading. To have the curls of a willing young woman tickling his face as they fucked, without needing to feel for her or worry how she felt, except that she felt wonderful as she rode him.

He pressed up and into Lilith again and she moaned. Success wasn't just about getting Grant to publish his novel. This was success—trying to time his thrusts so he and Lilith would come together. Getting the novel published was a way to get here, in her bed, pressed into her, hands sliding over her skin, pacing himself.

The sound of success wasn't applause. The sound of success was the sound he made as he thrust into her. That sound. He listened for it. The applause of her moans, the acclaim of her breathing. The clapping of their fucking. This was a beautiful thing they were writing together.

Lilith's flat abdomen was covered with sweat as it slid against his. She was laying right atop him now, sliding back and forth onto him. There was no review as perfect as how she was looking at him, into his eyes. No critique in any magazine could read him or his art so well. This was his best review. That look that came into her eyes, telling him she was about to disappear into an orgasm.

Every blink was more than a word.

When they came, together, arching, screaming, howling, tearing at one another, the work was complete, and there was no need for either of them to ruin it with essay or explanation. She fell asleep on top of him, with him still in her, and that was everything he needed to know of his success.

An hour into her sleep, he brushed a lock of her hair from her face, and she awoke with a tired smile, asking with her eyes if he was interested in more. He smiled back, but it was a smile of satisfaction with what they had already shared.

[...]

"As I said, you seem like an intelligent woman."

She laughed, and when she did, her curls again fell over her eyes. "When are you heading out of town?" she asked before kissing the tip of his nose.

"Three this afternoon," he replied.

"Plenty of time," she said before kissing him again.

From *Janus Incubus*, Chapter 48

THE PHYSICAL AND METAPHYSICAL

No exposition on sex, sexuality, and eroticism in fiction could be considered complete without a word on the spirituality of the sexual act. The term "to make love" has deep implications that go beyond its use as a euphemism for sexual intercourse. Lions, tigers, and bears *copulate*. If one believes, as I do, that human beings transcend their animalistic nature, that human beings can "be in love" at all, and that the physical union that occurs between two human beings in love can be much more than simply the insertion of a man's penis into a woman's vagina followed by sufficient movement to achieve orgasm, then surely one also believes that the author of serious fiction would be doing human beings a disservice by treating all sex in fiction as merely a collection of mechanical activities needing *only* mechanical technique to capture faithfully.

While it is possible to portray pure "fucking" between two characters, when that is what those two characters are indeed doing, it is also possible to convey a deeper metaphysical connection between two people who are exposing not only their bodies, but also their *souls* to one another during the act of sexual union.

As she opened up her legs under me, as my thighs touched the softness of her thighs, I felt my skin torn from me, until every tattoo, every piece of flesh I had covered with glyphs, every protective thing no longer was around me. Even though the lights were low, I could still see her eyes, and the fire there, and my fire reflected off them, illuminated her face.

I leaned with my neck, so that only my lips touched her, and our thighs touched hers, and her breasts barely touched my chest above her, but we touched at no other place. As she breathed, it went from her, into my mouth, and when I breathed, returned back to her. Like a serpent lit with oil, it slithered back and forth with a rhythm, until there was only one breathing. And when that soft rhythm had been perfectly attuned, I pressed my hips—just my hips and no other part of me—so that the tip of me was against her other lips.

My back screamed—Go in! My neck hollered—Now! My legs ached—Thrust! My lungs hurt so bad that each and every next breath absolutely depended on her to return air to me that I might breathe the next; for I had forgotten how to breathe any other way. I was waiting. Forcing myself to not push in. I was waiting for something ...

And then it came. She placed her right hand on the small of my back. While the sweat of her skin flowed into my sweat, an acid formed there, and started searing into my base chakra. I felt steel touch my skin. Cold relief. Slowly, as I mustered everything I had in my bone marrow to resist the first thrust, I waited as that steel slowly went past my skin, through the thin wall of muscle, and touched my spine. The cold tip on my spine carried all my pain up the blade, through the knife, up to her hand, and across the connection of the sweat.

To resist any longer was futile. Every agony in me was flying out my back and howling through the room, at my ears, trying to get back in, but not allowed back in. Like poltergeists, cursing, damning, even whispering sweet Siren promises of joy if let back in, but I listened only to Hannah's smell. That's what saved me from asking them to return.

And I pressed into her then, only when I knew those demons were on the run and could not return into me. Past her lips, into a warm place, against the most sensitive skin on me, I could feel her racing up my blade; her pains and demons, as the tip of me touched her closest and most desperately painful place.

The first thrust complete, I pulled back. It would have been murder to come out completely, so I waited just a moment when almost out, and returned for more.

A shower of acid and ice ripped through the roof of the room and bathed us both completely. Our skin was gone. Our muscle smoldering. Had it not been for the absolute electricity of our connection, we would have been killed.

Every thrust against her, every agony of our hips, every laceration of our brains, every garrote wire encircling our spines and the barbed wire around our hearts let loose. I felt death behind me, strangling me, trying to keep me from breathing Hannah's breath. Death is a jealous bitch, and the rage she showed my neck as I ignored her and thrust through and into Hannah had my blood pouring down my neck, onto my lover, but death could not get any of it on *her* hands.

And I knew that just behind Hannah, her death was slicing her and pulling at her and offering the same promises, sometimes sweetly, sometimes with unstopped rage. But Hannah was listening to me and what we had as we threw against one another, and as we twisted against our executioners' pull, she knew as well as I did that our only hope was to not let go of one another.

And then I felt it. It was in the special rhythm and desperation of her hips, and carried through to me and told my desperation it was safe to be released. That final pain, that final agony, that final prisoner inside, the one who always asks out of the box last. Like Pandora's Box, there was only one thing left: hope. And the only hope for lovers, the only true hope is the release of that last prisoner—Desperation.

With the tremor that started in her and carried through to me was the last release, the little death that always promises rebirth. Across the arc of my body, and through her, it shook and tore and shook some more. Every muscle in me tightened as every muscle in her did the same, and fire and brimstone against those two ancient cities stunk through and carried away everything. And that is when those angels of death, knowing they could not tear down our walls as long as we were together, left us be.

Completely and absolutely shattered, but able at last to live.

"Touched to the Bone"

In order to teach you *how* to write such fiction, I would also have to teach you what love *is*. I cannot teach you this. I can suggest, however, that you listen very closely to everything in your mind, body, and soul the next time you are in love and making love with that person with whom you feel such a love. Trying to capture that feeling, that moment, that spectacular event so that you may later write about it in your fiction is about as difficult as gathering moonbeams in a jar, but I suppose it's all really a matter of how badly you want to be able to sit down and tell the word, through your fiction, how vast and ineffable such a thing feels.

Other Considerations

This chapter shall tie up some loose ends on mechanics (including how to deal with ... *loose ends*).

SHOWING VERSUS TELLING

Everything was happening so oddly that she didn't feel a bit surprised at finding the Red Queen and the White Queen sitting close to her, one on each side: she would have liked very much to ask them how they came there, but she feared it would not be quite civil. However, there would be no harm, she thought, in asking if the game was over. "Please, would you tell me—" she began, looking timidly at the Red Queen.

—Lewis Carroll, *Through the Looking-Glass*

Let me tell you about James (not his real name!), a friend of mine. James is intelligent, witty, polite, and he respects the mother who bore him. James is also handsome, and a charming conversationalist, and so there are few women alive who would tell James to get lost were he to walk up to them and try to start a conversation with them. Not long ago, James and I got into an argument, and because he turned out to be right, I eventually conceded his point, and everything returned to peace and bliss in our friendship.

Bored *yet*? What I have done is just *tell* you all about James. You have probably not learned a thing at all about the man. What does it mean for James to be *intelligent* and *witty* and *handsome*? Nothing at all—you might not find his sense of humor to be witty one lick! As for his respect for his mother, who is to say that James' constantly giving in to his mother's wishes for him is born of respect? As for being handsome, now that is for the ladies to decide, is it not? I have reduced James to a collection of adjectives that might as well have been applied to a sentient bowl of fruit.

If I instead were to have told you of the time James sat through some of the most difficult university exams going, and came out with the highest scores, or of the time three men threatened to beat him up, and he managed to talk himself out of the fight, if I were to *show* you James and his mother in a typical conversation, then you might, upon reading the details of these things, come to some of the same conclusions that I have about James. If I were to give you a peek into five minutes of James' interactions with Jane, from her POV, you might see the effect the man can have on someone of the opposite sex. Were I to have relayed the details of the argument he and I had, and you read for yourself the rebuttal James offered me, and made your own decision that he was right and I was wrong, you would be far more impressed with James. He would be more than a few adjectives on a page.

So it is with showing and telling. It need not be about James, or any other character. If I tell you that the mountain outside my window is beautiful, you will have to take me on my word, and since you do not know what I find beautiful, you will have to fill in a lot of blanks about how the mountain *actually* looks.

Of course, sometimes narrative calls for telling rather than showing. Unimportant details can be quickly skipped over, if the narrative flow calls for it. Not *every* mountain seen out every window matters, and not every of James' miraculous attributes need be more than a quickly flashed adjective. It is your decision about what to show and what to tell, as dictated by the story at hand.

TITLES

A great story with a shoddy title is like a pretty face with a huge, hairy wart on the end of an otherwise perfect nose. I have always admired authors who can come up with titles such as "A Clean, Well-Lighted Place," "His Own, or Someone Else's Face," and "The Aurelian."

It has been my experience that journal and little editors do not typically ask that short story titles be changed,* and they very rarely offer suggestions for change. I sometimes wonder if an otherwise decent story has been rejected because of a sloppy title. It is thus much to my chagrin that editors are not in the habit of offering advice on this topic.

A good title, like a good character name, can add meaning to a story, but does so without giving away so much of the theme that the story's ending becomes clear within sentences of the opening. For instance, a story about a man hanging from a cliff saved by his hiking buddy's remembering he has a pocket knife stowed away in his left boot had best not be called, "The Pocket Knife" if the existence of a knife will clearly save the man the moment we read of his becoming entangled in his safety ropes. Something like "The Left Boot" might add some meaning to the story, but this meaning will only become clear *after* the buddy remembers the knife.

Sometimes, a very brief excerpt from dialog can make an effective title. For instance, the story "It Ain't Never Gonna Happen" begins as follows:

"It ain't never gonna happen. You won't ever be a novelist," he said over his newspaper. "You lack the discipline."

and ends as follows:

From the darkness, with a sheet pulled over his face like a newspaper, Mark replied, "I didn't write one. I guess I lack *discipline*. It ain't ever gonna happen."

"It Ain't Never Gonna Happen"

---

* In all, I have had editors ask twice for title changes in all of over fifty published short stories. "*La Danse Macabre*," became "Master D'Arcy's Protegéc" and "Slavery" became "Barefoot Sonata." In both cases, I consider the changed titles more appropriate for the reasons suggested by those editors.

The title of this story echoes the opening and closing quotations of the story, and also, since Mark *did indeed* write a novel that was destroyed, but refuses to tell Ken about it, the irony of the title is also clear.

Other titles can be somewhat more cryptic in their meaning. The story "Paladin" is about a man who seduces his best friend's wife to commit adultery with him, but who remains the man's friend and is not rejected because of it. The meaning of the world *paladin* in this context is "a trusted military leader (as for a medieval prince)," and we see through the story's progression that the interloper is, indeed, trusted with certain duties that the betrayed friend ought to have taken upon himself, rather than given to his "trusted military leader."

A title can have many meanings at the same time. "When a Stranger Wandered In" is a story about a stranger that wanders into a small American town and causes a bit of a stir by not just passing through, but it is ultimately also about a man who has had a stranger wander into his own body as the result of what he has seen during his service in France during World War Two. The second meaning of the title is made explicitly clear by the narrator himself at the end of the story:

> "A stranger wandered into my body when I went over there to fight, you understand? A stranger that none of them recognize anymore, and who doesn't recognize them. But I can look into strangers' eyes, and they mine, because they never knew me before. They don't know what color they were before they went different from all that...."
>
> **"When a Stranger Wandered In"**

Then there are the titles that probably mean nothing at all but sound interesting and do not take away anything, and so sit atop their story by default. Although the story "In the Shadow of Clay Pigeons" mentions clay pigeons and *The Shadow* radio program, and plays on the "who knows what evil lurks in the hearts of men," theme of the old radio program, the title itself is obscure in its *exact* meaning. At least it is to me, and I entitled the story. *Shhhh.* Don't tell anyone. Keep them guessing.

LOOSE ENDS

It is the loose ends with which men hang themselves.

—Zelda Fitzgerald

If your fiction asks a question, but doesn't provide the reader with any kind of answer (or means to arriving at an answer), it has left a loose end.

Some character may have entered the story, gotten close to the protagonist, and then simply disappeared without a trace. Readers will ask themselves, "Whatever happened to …?" Perhaps what happened is that you wanted to carry that character further, but simply ran out of steam and focused on other characters. Life is like that anyway, right? People come, spend a few hours, get really close, and then simply disappear. Yes, life is like that, and yes, fiction is supposed to be modeled after life. Nonetheless, carelessness or haste in one's fiction is taken by many readers to be a sign of disrespect for them and the form. Some doors must be closed if we wish to keep the winds of readers' discontent from blowing away the full impact our fiction might have made.

How to tie off such loose ends? One option is to remove the start of the string, leaving no end. If some character comes, builds, and then vanishes, you always have the option to remove that character from the narrative altogether, or merge that character with another who didn't simply vanish. The reader will never know that what is presented as a single character was once two, and the loose end of the ship that passed too quickly in the night will magically vanish from view.

This strategy allows you to avoid a silly denouement passage later on in the story:

"Whatever happened to Jane?" Bob asked.

"I heard she got hit by a bus," John replied.

"Damned shame, you two seemed to be getting along famously well," Bob said.

"Yup. Win some, lose some, eh?"

Forced Closure

Some loose ends are not so much loose ends as they are open questions. If this is your intention as an artist, rather than an accident of construction, you are less likely to annoy the reader. Fake it, or try to pass off haste as some kind of profundity, however, and you may find your work hangs itself on the loose ends.

Part 2: Aesthetics

Don't waste yourself in rejection, nor bark against the bad, but chant the beauty of the good.

—Ralph Waldo Emerson

Beyond the mechanical issues of fiction are the aesthetic considerations. When one speaks of character movement, symbol and allusions, and theme, one is entering less clearly charted territory than when one speaks of point of view, dialog, and tense, and indeed, aesthetic issues are less easily defined, but are of critical importance in serious fiction.

First, let me explain exactly what I mean to do when I hold aesthetics up as being something different from mechanics. Aesthetics are about the beauty behind a story, and by beauty, I do not mean prettiness or preciousness. I consider Camus' novel *L'Étranger* (*The Outsider*) and Knut Hamsun's *Sult* (*Hunger*) to be aesthetically pleasing novels, but neither is about anything particularly pleasing to the senses in the way a bucket of ice cream on a field of fresh grass on a hot summer's day might be pleasing. These novels are pleasing because they examine human nature carefully, honestly, and do so in a way that is enjoyable—in a very broad sense—for me to read. In short, they are aesthetically masterful works because they are, in my opinion, beautiful art, even in the face of their dark subject matter.

Well-orchestrated mechanics are a large part of literary aesthetics, but they are not enough unto themselves. The most brilliantly turned phrase, most authentic dialog, and the most tightly knit plot, without much under the surface to say to a reader, are like what finely polished glass is when compared to finely polished diamond. A quick jerk of the mental hammer will shatter the glass, but do no harm to the diamond. A work that is perfectly executed, but has nothing of merit to say—a piece that puts form before substance—is, at best, a temporary joy waiting for a hammer stroke to shatter it.

Works that dig under the skin of the human condition by exposing genuine and meaningful character movement, speak to humanity through theme, evoke timeless allusions, and leave one with more understanding than before one read them, however, are something to behold, even if they are not perfectly executed on a mechanical level. The ideal, of course, is to produce works that are both mechanically *and* aesthetically superior. An author may never be able to reach that mark, but can still strive towards it.

Character Movement

"Who are *you*?" said the Caterpillar.

This was not an encouraging opening for a conversation. Alice replied, rather shyly, "I—I hardly know, sir, just at present—at least I know who I WAS when I got up this morning, but I think I must have been changed several times since then."

—Lewis Carroll, *Alice in Wonderland*

The mechanics of "character" have already been discussed, but the aesthetics of character take into account something less tangible than the factors already mentioned. The measure of a character's uniqueness and verisimilitude is the distance that character is moved by the events and happenings of the story.

That is to say, a real character is not merely someone who consists of a collection of attributes arranged such that they are just so, but rather, someone who, at a unique moment in fictional time, is presented with an opportunity for change and either moves forward, backward, or makes a conscious decision to go nowhere at all. This degree of opportunity and the degree of actualization of this opportunity are what makes a character in a piece unique; never again will all of the pieces, all of the motivations, all of the events be in just such a configuration, and how the character responds is something that can never be reproduced in any other story, time, or place.

It should go without saying that a conscientious author will have set up the circumstances for change in such a manner that the character movement made will be consistent with the entirety of the piece. Just because the outcome is inevitable, however, does not mean that it need be apparent before it actually occurs; the reader ought to be able to say of the movement afterwards, "This is what was *meant* to be—what suited the character best—even if I didn't see it coming."

What exactly *is* character movement?

In the story "Fractures," an aging Muslim man wakes up, says his morning prayer, steps onto his porch to gather the fruit left by a local boy, returns to his room, looks to his cat, and makes an observation about his own invariant routine:

> "You know, Gris, if someone wanted to poison me, all they would have to do is figure out that Mahmet leaves a piece of fruit for me every morning. I'd be easy to poison. Creature of habit. Full of fractures."
>
> Gris didn't care. She just scratched the floor under her claws, pushed her nose into Ahmet Bey's callused hand, and accepted what she could get.

"Fractures"

That Ahmet Bey *realizes* his life has become fractured and stagnant, but voluntarily elects to continue in the cycle *is* the movement. How can it be that deciding to go nowhere is considered movement? People continue on with what they have always been doing all the time. How often, though, do people have an epiphany about their inactivity, and then consciously elect to remain in stasis? Ahmet Bey's character has *moved* more closely to solidity. This decision to remain in his cycle after coming to a realization about his life is what makes him unlike any other character in any other story, unlike any other aging Muslim man in any other one room apartment in Istanbul.

More often, of course, movement does not involve the decision to stay where one already is. In the story "In the Shadow of Clay Pigeons," the young protagonist Mark maims his best friend through his own carelessness. When another boy takes a beating in the adults' attempt to find out who has maimed the friend, Mark is presented with an opportunity to go to the adults and confess that he is the one who did the deed.

Mark can go in two directions as a character: he can grow more responsible for his own actions and admit what he has done, or he can grow more cowardly, and run away from his responsibility for his friend's accident:

"He tried to beat it out of me," Ritchie finally said.

Mark's heart was beating hard.

"Jesus," Mark finally managed to say.

"I didn't say nothing," Ritchie then said. "Got it? Nothing."

Mark and Ritchie started walking along the sea.

"Is he going to be all right?" Mark asked. The sea was spraying at his shoes.

"My dad says probably not," Ritchie said. "Maybe if the plane got here sooner, but it took a long time to get him to the hospital."

They did not speak after that. Mark plunged his hands into the icy seawater and shook them about. "You know...," he began. [...] That night, Mark did not sleep well.

The next day, he did not come out of the trailer at all. The hours passed, and he just stayed in his bed, unable to move.

At about two in the afternoon, his mother arrived at his bedroom door. "Bill's mom radioed in to Sharon," she said. Her voice was heavy.

Mark sat up and looked at his mother.

"The doctors got it out of his head, but Billy nearly died," she said.

Mark closed his eyes and fell back onto his pillow. He could not think much.

"She says they say he probably will never be the same. Almost a vegetable, they say. He was such a bright boy before all this," she added as she closed the door.

Like a clay pigeon, Bill had disappeared in an instant.

Ten minutes' of tears streamed down Mark's cheeks before his door opened and his mother again walked into the room. She sat on the side of his bed and took his hand into hers, slowing caressing it. She brushed his hair from over his closed eyes. He could feel her fingers smooth away the tears, as she leaned over and kissed his forehead.

"I'm just glad it wasn't you," she whispered.

Mark wanted to say to his mother, "But it *was* me," but he could not open his mouth.

"I'm very sad for Billy's mom, but if that had been you with that in your head, I don't know what I would do now." She then stood, closed the door, and left Mark alone.

Mark did not get out of bed. The time came that he normally would have turned on his radio and listened to the radio plays, but he did not do that this night, for the first time in months. This Saturday night passed slowly through the guilt-ridden heat. Only the shadows and horseflies knew what lurked in his heart. The sea had not taken away the stains from the hands of a ten-year-old boy. Unlike clay pigeons, the stains would not disappear when he opened his eyes.

"In the Shadow of Clay Pigeons"

At what point in the above narrative is it clear that Mark's growth is towards cowardice? When he plunges his hands into the sea after hearing that his friend Ritchie had taken a beating to protect the identity of the boy who injured Bill. When Mark's mother later shows her concern, he could confess, but his character has already moved towards remaining silent on the matter.

An altogether different kind of character movement occurs in the story "Staircases." At the beginning of this story, Nolan is saved from suicide by drowning by Lloyd, a young widower. The two young men form a bond, and Nolan decides to join Lloyd on a quest into the mountains of Northern India with the goal of depositing Lloyd's deceased wife's diary in a Buddhist temple in the Himalayas.

As the story progresses, Lloyd becomes very ill as the ultimate result of having earlier dived into the polluted Seine to save Nolan. Because they are alone in the hills, Lloyd cannot be saved, and dies in Nolan's arms. Throughout this story, Nolan moves from being a self-concerned, suicidal youth, to being more concerned about the life of another than his own.

He is able to do this because, as he puts it just before the fateful trek into the mountains:

He had done more than jump into the cold waters of the Seine to pull me back to myself. Even with a persistent cough from having sucked in a bit of the Seine, he had helped me track down Anne-Jolie, and comforted me during the week afterwards when I recovered from her speech about how she and I could never again see one another. He read my stories when I wrote them, and faithfully posted them for me even when I did not have the courage to send them to publishers. Had he been a woman, I probably would have loved him, so I did not judge him too harshly for his temper.

In the way one man can love another, I did love Lloyd Kirk. I loved the way he was able to stare at me, in his uniquely determined way, and get me to stop [fooling] myself about life. I often wished I had his clarity of purpose, his single minded innocence, his total lack of self-pity. I could love him in that way, temper or not, and I tried to show him that I did by agreeing to everything he proposed. That was how Lloyd wanted to be loved: with absolute loyalty—and I tried to give him that—even when he drank himself stupid and started hurling curses at the world. Perhaps it was a better love than any love I could have for a woman, because it was a love I could have that didn't constantly require me to also love myself and have that love—and myself—put to the question.

[...] I was becoming his brother.

"Staircases"

Because Nolan's character has moved from self-concern to concern for another, he has become more than himself, as symbolized in his waking up the moment Lloyd dies near the end of the story:

"Nolan," he said, very weakly an hour later.
"Yes?"
"You owe me your life," he said.
"I know." I started to sob. I owed him more than my life.
"Will you make good on that?" he asked. His mouth barely moved as he spoke. "Nothing ever dies up here. I don't want her diary to die."
"Nothing and nobody will die," I said.
Before he fell back asleep, he moved his lips and said something that I could not make out. Finally, he was asleep again. I crawled into his blankets and held his burning body close to mine. I didn't want him to be alone. So close to him, I could feel him inhale and exhale, although his breaths were very shallow. I awoke, then, when he stopped breathing completely.

"Staircases"

Not all character movement occurs within the scope of the narrative itself. In "When a Stranger Wandered In,"

101

Adrian Lafontaine's movement has already occurred during Lafontaine's military service in France. The war is already over and the protagonist has already been moved to find a town almost exactly like his hometown, but populated by strangers.

This decision, despite its having been made outside the timeline of the story itself, is the driving motivation behind his actions during the narrative, and culminates in his final disclosure at the close of the story:

Adrian put his hand again on the innkeeper's shoulder. "But you see, sir, when you go away ... and see so much ... so much death and destruction, it changes you. Inside. It changes your eyes. You can look in my eyes, and it won't matter, you understand? It won't matter to you, because you're a stranger. You never knew me before I went to war. Someone like Susan Brown can look into my eyes, and maybe take a fancy to me. Maybe want me to ask her to dance."

"Supposing you're properly introduced," Mr. Coppersmith said, poking Adrian in the ribs lightly and grinning.

"Yes. Supposing we're properly introduced," he agreed, grinning back. "Mrs. Trent and Mrs. Macdonald can look into these eyes and see a decent young man who served his country and came back alive in mostly working order. A stranger with an honorable past and a decent idea for the future. But nobody over in Willowbrook, my hometown, can do that now. They remember the old eyes. The eyes that never looked into a dying man's face and shoved the bayonet a little harder. The eyes that never saw someone all of sixteen years of age die three feet from them. You understand? They can't look into these eyes, and I can't look into theirs. Not anymore. It's cold and it's chilling. You understand? Like you've never felt, I assure you.

"A stranger wandered into my body when I went over there to fight, you understand? A stranger that none of them recognize anymore, and who doesn't recognize them. But I can look into strangers' eyes, and they mine, because they never knew me before. They don't know what color they were before they went different from all that. I still remember what I loved about the small town life. That the bastards couldn't steal from me. So I want that back. That little piece of apple pie they couldn't steal from me. I can build from there."

"When a Stranger Wandered In"

Symbol & Allusion

"When *I* use a word," Humpty Dumpty said, in rather a scornful tone, "it means just what I choose it to mean—neither more nor less."

"The question is," said Alice, "whether you *can* make words mean so many different things."

"The question is," said Humpty Dumpty, "which is to be master—that's all."

—Lewis Carroll, *Through the Looking-Glass*

In fiction, all may not be what it at first appears to be; it may be much more. The use of symbol in storytelling is as old as the craft itself, and for good reason. Symbols speak to us in ways that words alone sometimes do not; they get past our mental defenses and speak to us even when we are not prepared to listen. Allusion, on the other hand, attempts to speak to us by compressing the message in one piece into a hint about where the fuller message may be found. Used sparingly and when genuinely called for, symbol and allusion used in concert can add layers to a story that give it new meaning on the fifth and sixth readings.

SYMBOL

What is a symbol? The simplest definition is that a symbol is something that stands for or represents something else through some (sometimes tenuous) association. That association can come from many origins: cultural past, religious heritage, implied societal norms, or even clichés that are so much rooted in truth (or just so often repeated) that they have become symbolic in meaning.

Consider this passage from "In the Shadow of Clay Pigeons":

"Stand about ten feet behind us, kids," Duke said as he took the gun from Richard.

Richard stepped back a few paces from his friend. Ritchie pulled back the arm of the launcher, placed a clay pigeon on it, and waited.

Duke closed his eyes, as if thinking, and then yelled out, "Pull!" and the pigeon went flying. A second later, Duke opened his eyes, and the pigeon was gone.

"That looks fun!" Sean called out.

"Pretty neat, hey?" Richard called out.

"Open your eyes one second after you hear me yell *pull*," Duke said.

A few moments later, Duke yelled the command, and Mark counted one, and opened his eyes. The disk in the sky disappeared into dust.

"In the Shadow of Clay Pigeons"

In the above passage, from a story in which a young boy accidentally maims his best friend, the destruction of the clay pigeons represents the frailty of human beings, and the act of closing one's eyes and then opening them to the destruction represents the dangers of carelessness. That humans are often compared to clay, and keeping one's eyes open is a metaphor for being careful, have religious and social roots. Although it would have been possible to have had one character say to another, "Human beings are frail creatures," the use of symbols to express this idea carries the same message at a deeper level than mere words of dialog or narrative.

Symbols can also be manufactured for the purpose of the piece itself, which is to say that something can take on a symbolic meaning that it might not have except in the fictional piece. If some object is found in one scene, and then again later in another, that object may be a symbol. This device can also be used to echo back to the first passage, or it may take on a meaning that is specific to the piece.

For instance, in the novel *Janus Incubus*, the protagonist buys a mandolin necklace made by a Gypsy character named Jacques:

> I shuffled up to a street vendor and, as I looked over his pieces, I saw a small, brass mandolin on a necklace. The workmanship seemed familiar. I turned the charm around, and saw the unmistakable mark of Jacques the Basque. No two were alike. This was his work.
>
> Was he here, too? I knew that summer was his season for Montreal. The cold of winter had passed, and he could migrate east again, where the action was. If Jacques the Basque would be anywhere, he would be in Old Montreal. I guessed that he would be hiding in the respite of the shade of an alley or side street. He had worn black every time I saw him and, in such a bright place as this, he would be off to the side to keep out of the sunshine.
>
> "Do you know a Basque vendor named Jacques?" I asked a street vendor.
>
> "Jacques? A Basque?" he said, reaching over to a necklace that had a mandolin on it. He put the necklace against my chest. "Nice on you," he said, admiring the exquisite handiwork of the piece. "Do I know a Jacques? No."
>
> I paid him the fifteen dollars asked for the necklace and started across to the street to the next nearest vendor, a man called Yves. "Do you know of a Basque vendor named Jacques?" I asked. I showed him the mark on the back of the charm.
>
> He screwed up his eyes. "Ah, yes, Jacques the Basque! I know him! We all know him. He goes back and forth across the country with the seasons. A *real* gypsy! Great work! Does it all himself. No cheap import crap."

From *Janus Incubus*, Chapter 26

This necklace somehow finds itself on Mark's neck in the last chapter of the novel, at the moment he recognizes someone from his Montreal days, even though it has long since been lost to time, since he last put that necklace around the neck of a dead man whose identity he had assumed. Since the closing passages of the novel are included later in this chapter, I shall leave it to the reader to decide what the symbol means.

Another such manufactured symbol finds itself in the novel *Abadoun*. In this novel, a young boy steals a single tomato, and as punishment, receives thirty lashes from the shopkeeper whose tomato he stole.

The protagonist of the novel, in an attempt to assuage his conscience for his role in capturing the thief who is then so cruelly punished, offers the boy one *tuman* for every lash.

> "How many tomatoes were in that pile, boy?" someone asked. I saw that it was the city man who had caught me. I was not afraid of him.
>
> "Thirty," I answered as boldly as I could muster.
>
> "You survived *thirty* lashes?"
>
> "Every one of them!" I returned, thinking, *I am a khan, son of a khan, grandson of a khan!*
>
> The city man searched through his pocket. "Here is one *tuman* for every lash," he explained as he handed the money to me. "Go to *Peiman-e-Omar* and buy something to eat there. The oven should be hot, so you will warm up a bit."

From *Abadoun*, Chapter 10

The novel ends with the sentence, "And a man driving to Saqqez had thought, *How much are tomatoes worth in America?*"

The symbol of the one tomato and the money paid for the lashes tie to the novel's main conflict: should the protagonist go to Teheran on his mission to save one political prisoner, or stay in the town of Abadoun and save that entire town of villagers from certain gassing? The "one tomato" then, symbolizes the political prisoner, and the cost of saving the town is represented by the money paid.

ALLUSION

Allusion is another device used to express deeper meaning than first appears on the surface of the narrative. Near the end of the same story, young Mark plunges his hands into sea water in order to wash them clean. When considered in light of Mark's responsibility for his friend's accident, this is clearly an allusion to the Biblical account of Pontius Pilate's washing his hands clean of responsibility for Jesus' crucifixion. Because the story of Pilate's role in Jesus' death is well known in Judeo-Christian influenced literature, a simple reference to Mark's washing his hands suffices to conjure many deeper implications for the story, captured in only a single clause of a sentence.

Allusion can occur in a character's name. For instance, in the short story "The Revenge of Clarlucia Verdadez," the name of the headmistress of Clarlucia's school is Señora Delasmoscas, which, when translated to English, roughly means "Lady of the Flies."

The story has several passages where flies circle the headmistress's head, and concludes as follows:

> That night, Señora Milagrosa Delasmoscas went to sleep after a heavy meal and dreamed of her retirement. When she awoke the next morning, she felt that her head weighed more than it had the night before. She stumbled to her Looking-Glass as she did every morning and whined loudly when she saw her reflection there.
>
> To her great shock and terror, the Headmistress of *Santa Maria en las Montañas* had the head of a great, black boar.

"The Revenge of Clarlucia Verdadez"

The Lord of the Flies is an allusion to the demon Beelzebub. That her head should be transformed to that of a boar, then, is fitting with the connection so made.

Allusion can also occur when an author invokes another's (or his own) work in an attempt to compress meaning into the present work. In the novel *Janus Incubus*, is the following passage:

> Take a man you claim to desire and, when he rejects you because you do not allow him to be himself, put him in boiling oil, or put him out in the cold to have the heat of his soul spill out into the crispness of the outside world. When all of his heat has left him, throw a bucket of ice water on him so that the only thing he has left

to save his life, to keep that little bit of heat inside that keeps his heart pounding, is the blanket he won't sell to anyone. Let him, like Hamsun's starving idiot, scream at Jesus and curse God and die. No, I did not curse God that day, but instead prayed and screamed to Him, not against Him. Job, not Hamsun's moron.

From *Janus Incubus*, Chapter 10

The above passage actually has two allusions: one literary and one Biblical. The reference to "the blanket he won't sell to anyone" is an allusion to a situation in Knut Hamsun's *Hunger*. The protagonist of *Hunger* is starving, and having put into pawn everything he owns, refuses to put into pawn a blanket lent to him by someone else, on principle, until he has reached absolute rock bottom:

Now I was to die. It was in the time of the fall, and all things were hushed to sleep. I had tried every means, exhausted every resource of which I knew. I fondled this thought sentimentally, and each time I still hoped for a possible succour I whispered repudiatingly: "You fool, you have already begun to die."

I ought to write a couple of letters, make all ready—prepare myself. I would wash myself carefully and tidy my bed nicely. I would lay my head upon the sheets of white paper, the cleanest things I had left, and the green blanket. I … The green blanket! Like a shot I was wide awake. The blood mounted to my head, and I got violent palpitation of the heart. I arise from the seat, and start to walk. Life stirs again in all my fibres, and time after time I repeat disconnectedly, "The green blanket—the green blanket." I go faster and faster, as if it is a case of fetching something, and stand after a little time in my tinker's workshop. Without pausing a moment, or wavering in my resolution, I go over to the bed, and roll up Hans Pauli's blanket. It was a strange thing if this bright idea of mine couldn't save me. I rose infinitely superior to the stupid scruples which sprang up in me—half inward cries about a certain stain on my honour. I bade good-bye to the whole of them. I was no hero—no virtuous idiot. I had my senses left.

So I took the blanket under my arm and went to No. 5 Stener's Street. I knocked, and entered the big, strange room for the first time. The bell on the door above my head gave a lot of violent jerks. A man enters from a side room, chewing, his mouth is full of food, and stands behind the counter.

"Eh, lend me sixpence on my eye-glasses?" said I. "I shall release them in a couple of days, without fail—eh?"

"No! they're steel, aren't they?"

"Yes."

"No; can't do it."

"Ah, no, I suppose you can't. Well, it was really at best only a joke. Well, I have a blanket with me for which, properly speaking, I have no longer any use, and it struck me that you might take it off my hands."

"I have—more's the pity—a whole store full of bed-clothes," he replied; and when I had opened it he just cast one glance over it and said, "No, excuse me, but I haven't any use for that either."

"I wanted to show you the worse side first," said I; "it's much better on the other side."

"Ay, ay; it's no good. I won't own it; and you wouldn't raise a penny on it anywhere."

"No, it's clear it isn't worth anything," I said; "but I thought it might go with another old blanket at an auction."

"Well, no; it's no use."

"Three pence?" said I.

"No; I won't have it at all, man! I wouldn't have it in the house!" I took it under my arm and went home.

I acted as if nothing had passed, spread it over the bed again, smoothed it well out, as was my custom, and tried to wipe away every trace of my late action. I could not possibly have been in my right mind at the moment when I came to the conclusion to commit this rascally trick. The more I thought over it the more unreasonable it seemed to me. It must have been an attack of weakness; some relaxation in my inner self that had surprised me when off my guard. Neither had I fallen straight into the trap. I had half felt that I was going the wrong road, and I expressly offered my glasses first, and I rejoiced greatly that I had not had the opportunity of carrying into effect this fault which would have sullied the last hours I had to live.

From *Hunger*, Part II

Hunger's protagonist, however, *does* curse God, which Mark refuses to do, even though he is in a similar situation at this point in his life. Thus, the reference to "Job, not Hamsun's moron" is that he will not curse God, even though he is suffering terribly.

2:9 Then said his wife unto him, Dost thou still retain thine integrity? curse God, and die. 2:10 But he said unto her, Thou speakest as one of the foolish women speaketh. What? shall we receive good at the hand of God, and shall we not receive evil? In all this did not Job sin with his lips.

The Book of Job 2:9-10 (KJV)

The deepest meaning of this passage in *Janus Incubus* can only be determined by reading *Hunger*, since to fully understand the desperation Mark feels himself facing, one must understand the identification he feels between himself and the protagonist of that novel, especially his rejection by the love interest. This identification between mark and Hamsun's character from *Hunger* returns later in the novel, through further use of allusion:

I read the simple signed "With respect and love" on the inside, and accepted the gift with a smile. "I appreciate this," I said. I did appreciate it. [...]

"What are you up to these days other than working here?" she asked. "It's so different from *La Farfalla*."

"Not really," I said, flipping through the pages of *Caligula*. "Here, I must know the value of a literary gem, instead of a bracelet, is all." I put the book under the counter. "The surplus value is still what keeps the shop open."

"Say, could we...?" she started. She did not have to finish her question for me to know what she wanted to say. Why did she have to go and ruin what could have been a nice conclusion to everything that had happened?

"Do you know what I've called you? *Ylajali*. Now, from all these books, find me the one book that will tell you what that means, and I'd consider it, after you read it through." I felt a deep satisfaction in saying this.

"Ylajali?"

"Yes," I said. It was perfect. "Ee-la-*ya*-lee. It sounds so sweet on the tongue, doesn't it?"

From *Janus Incubus*, Chapter 19

Ylajali is the name Hamsun's protagonist gives to the woman he has fallen for in the novel. Mark knows that Vanessa will never find *Hunger* in the store, and thus knows he will never again be with her. Hamsun's passage reads:

> I stopped, and let her pass ahead again. I could, for the moment, go no further; the whole thing struck me as being so singular. I was in a tantalizing mood, annoyed with myself on account of the pencil incident, and in a high degree disturbed by all the food I had taken on a totally empty stomach. Suddenly my thoughts, as if whimsically inspired, take a singular direction. I feel myself seized with an odd desire to make this lady afraid; to follow her, and annoy her in some way. I overtake her again, pass her by, turn quickly round, and meet her face-to-face in order to observe her well. I stand and gaze into her eyes, and hit, on the spur of the moment, on a name which I have never heard before—a name with a gliding, nervous sound—Ylajali! When she is quite close to me I draw myself up and say impressively:
>
> "You are losing your book, madam!" I could hear my heart beat audibly as I said it.
>
> "My book?" she asks her companion, and she walks on.
>
> My devilment waxed apace, and I followed them. At the same time, I was fully conscious that I was playing a mad prank without being able to stop myself. My disordered condition ran away with me; I was inspired with the craziest notions, which I followed blindly as they came to me. I couldn't help it, no matter how much I told myself that I was playing the fool. I made the most idiotic grimaces behind the lady's back, and coughed frantically as I passed her by. Walking on in this manner—very slowly, and always a few steps in advance—I felt her eyes on my back, and involuntarily put down my head with shame for having caused her annoyance. By degrees, a wonderful feeling stole over me of being far, far away in other places; I had a half-undefined sense that it was not I who was going along over the gravel hanging my head.
>
> A few minutes later, they reached Pascha's bookshop. I had already stopped at the first window, and as they go by I step forward and repeat:
>
> "You are losing your book, madam!"
>
> "No; what book?" she asks affrightedly. "Can you make out what book it is he is talking about?" and she comes to a stop.

I hug myself with delight at her confusion; the irresolute perplexity in her eyes positively fascinates me. Her mind cannot grasp my short, passionate address. She has no book with her; not a single page of a book, and yet she fumbles in her pockets, looks down repeatedly at her hands, turns her head and scrutinizes the streets behind her, exerts her sensitive little brain to the utmost in trying to discover what book it is I am talking about. Her face changes colour, has now one, now another expression, and she is breathing quite audibly—even the very buttons on her gown seem to stare at me, like a row of frightened eyes.

From *Hunger*, Part I

The true (or at least, fuller) *meaning* of the allusion in *Janus Incubus*, again, can only be ascertained if the reader has also read *Hunger*. In a sense, then, allusion is an act that involves the author of a piece of fiction tapping on the reader's shoulder and sharing a secret about the meaning of the piece, just as Mark is offering to share what he has learned about his relationship with Vanessa with her, if she only finds and reads the alluded to work.

That is, the confusion Mark creates (and the satisfaction he feels by doing so) by his reference to Ylajali, and the confusion of the character in Hamsun's passage are connected, at least in Mark's mind.

Allusion can also occur through style. A piece of work may imitate some other work so closely that it calls to the reader's attention that other work, but only through the way in which it is written.

In *Janus Incubus*, chapter 24 ends and chapter 25 begins in a way that points the reader to Jack London's *Martin Eden*:

After Hans left, I was able to keep my mind on track, and managed to reread through the first half of *Martin Eden* without losing focus. I was on the third paragraph of chapter twenty when the phone rang. It was Vanessa.

"I found the book," she announced proudly.

"So quickly?" I said.

"I cheated," she admitted. "I phoned up a librarian the next morning. Took her about ten minutes to figure it out."

"Did you read the book?" I asked. I reread the third paragraph of chapter twenty again.

"Only very quickly," she said. "The English translation, anyway."

"And?"

"You're too damned complicated," she said, laughing. "But I do think I can see now how I made you feel and I am sorry."

"'The moon had not yet risen,'" I cited a line from what I was reading.

"Pardon?"

"Oh, nothing," he said. "Contemplating being ruthless," I said.

"You're too damned complicated," she repeated herself. She and I chatted a short while longer, until we finally both hung up at the same time. I proceeded to the next chapter.

CHAPTER 25

Came a horrible summer day, warm and humid, putrid with the divided east and west of the deranging season, a Montreal summer day, with crazy sun and thundering whips of breeze that did not stir the strangle of the air.

From *Janus Incubus*, Chapters 24 and 25

Here, the allusion is practically a citation: the third paragraph of chapter twenty of *Martin Eden* reads as follows:

But Ruth laughed from security. She was sure of herself, and in a few days he would be off to sea. Then, by the time he returned, she would be away on her visit East. There was a magic, however, in the strength and health of Martin. He, too, had been told of her contemplated Eastern trip, and he felt the need for haste. Yet he did not know how to make love to a girl like Ruth. Then, too, he was handicapped by the possession of a great fund of experience with girls and women who had been absolutely different from her. They had known about love and life and flirtation, while she knew nothing about such things. Her prodigious innocence appalled him, freezing on his lips all ardors of speech, and convincing him, in spite of himself, of his own unworthiness. Also he was handicapped in another way. He had himself never been in love before. He had liked women in that turgid past of his, and been fascinated by some of them, but he had not known what it was to love them. He had whistled in a masterful, careless way, and they had come to him. They had been diversions, incidents, part of the game men play, but a small part at most. And now, and for the first time, he was a suppliant, tender and timid and doubting. He did not know the way of love, nor its speech, while he was frightened at his loved one's clear innocence.

From *Martin Eden*, Chapter 20

So, when Mark plays with words and says he is contemplating being *ruth*less, what he is really saying (given the allusion to the above passage from *Martin Eden*), is that is contemplating what life will be like without the woman he loves.

Is there further allusion? Yes. The *style* (right down to the syntax) of the first sentence of the "next chapter" of *Janus Incubus* is borrowed directly from the first sentence of the next chapter (21) of *Martin Eden*, which can be seen here:

Came a beautiful fall day, warm and languid, palpitant with the hush of the changing season, a California Indian summer day, with hazy sun and wandering wisps of breeze that did not stir the slumber of the air.

From *Martin Eden*, Chapter 20

I mentioned in Part 1 that the most influential novel ending I've ever read is the ending of *Martin Eden*. Here is the ending of *Janus Incubus*:

Down, down, down, spinning, dancing down the staircase, finally coming to the mountain road. Cohen Benjamin was there, on the pass, with Marie-Claire, waving at me, smiling. The snow had all melted. It was the trekking season.

—There are no walls here, Mark!

Much further down the road was a third person I could not make out.

I strained to see who the third person was. I ran past Cohen and Marie-Claire, who had their arms open wide to greet me. A mandolin bounced on the necklace on my chest. I hadn't seen that necklace since I put it around Cohen's neck at the *gompa*. Was that third person *Abel*? When the darkness came, at that very instant, I both knew, and could know no more.

Last Chapter of *Janus Incubus*

The reference to the interminable staircase and the similarity of the last sentences are clear, and intentional.

There is, in the context of *Janus Incubus*, a reason "Mark" recognizes "Abel" in the last paragraph of the novel. The name "Abel" and its relation to "Mark" and an earlier passage in the novel are, in fact, Biblical allusions to the story of Cain and Abel.

> I wanted out of the place. It was not the bookstore I knew. The heat was suffocating, but it was not that alone. It was Abel. Had I been Cain, I would have picked up a heavy book and clubbed him with it. There was nothing wrong with his *writing*. I supposed it deserved to be in the journal. I loathed him not because the gods had found his sacrifice more righteous than mine—after all, I had never put my lamb before the gods, and could admit to myself that his lamb was fatter—but because he was the gargoyle on the cover. I could take no more, and returned to my search.
>
> —Do you have *The Sun Also Rises*? I interrupted his impromptu lecture on whatever it was exactly he was saying.
>
> —Hemingway? That would be in the A.D.W. Section, he said. Another Dead Writer, he explained.
>
> I could feel my blood rising into my face. My heart was pounding. I searched my brain for one quotation, anything, that I could use to club him. Nothing came to me. I did not reply, but simply went about looking for the book. I could not find it, and walked briskly out of the place, without another word. I expected him to bid me leave, but Abel was not speaking.
>
> I wiped my nose, thinking that it was running from the heat. Blood. Damn it, I had a nose bleed. I had gotten so angry at Abel that my nose was bleeding profusely. It was everywhere on my hands.

From *Janus Incubus*, Chapter 31

How far can an author carry such allusions? As far as he dares, but no further.

Res Ipsa Loquitur

Yes, the work "speaks for itself." Sometimes it speaks clearly, sometimes it mumbles, stutters, or whispers, and sometimes the batteries in our hearing aids are dead.

—Fred Candelaria

By explaining my intent when writing so many pieces in this book, I have broken the rule that writers ought not explain too much. After all, the work is supposed to speak for itself. As already mentioned in the introduction, however, I felt it would have been a greater sin to invent the motivations and intent behind other authors' works, and try to pass off my interpretations as truth about that intent.

There are areas of fiction, however, where only the work truly can speak for itself: theme and style. Theme because, well, sometimes theme arises differently for one reader than for another, no matter the author's intent, and style because it is also often outside the author's control. Some authors have a style, without ever having intended to have any style at all. Indeed, some authors consider *intentionally* writing in a particular way to be a cardinal sin. I shall not, then, comment on the themes or style of my own works, except to tell you what others have said of my style.

This does not, however, mean that theme and style cannot be discussed herein.

THEME

"What do you mean by that?" said the Caterpillar sternly. "Explain yourself!"

"I can't explain *myself*, I'm afraid, sir" said Alice, "because I'm not myself, you see."

"I don't see," said the Caterpillar.

"I'm afraid I can't put it more clearly," Alice replied very politely, "for I can't understand it myself to begin with...."

—Lewis Carroll, *Alice in Wonderland*

When you read a story and come out of the experience with a succinct revelation about life, honed in your mind by the totality of the story, you have come out of that story sensing its *theme*. If the protagonist's actions in the face of danger or difficulty left you able to say, "The author of this piece meant to expose the falsehood that _____," you have encountered *theme*.

Even were I able to nail a definition of theme squarely on the head, it is unlikely that I could offer any tangible suggestions about how to work with theme in your own work. Why? Because theme ultimately (or at least ideally) emerges from the sum of all the parts of a story as they interact with one another with the reader, and only you can orchestrate all of the many various parts of your own work in your attempt to convey theme to a reader. Only you can repeat a line or two of dialog at the right time, with the right emphasis, after putting a ray of light onto the right symbol, near the right allusion, with a story given the right title, with the right beginning, middle, and ending, such that the theme of the story shines forth to *your* readers' eyes.

What I can say about theme is that it is not the moral of the story. Some themes will, indeed, be moralistic, and certainly your views on life will have some bearing on the classes of theme that you investigate in your fiction. If you view life as an absurd collection of barely connected events, or conversely, as an interwoven series of deity-directed machinations, the themes you convey through your stories may reflect this view. If you believe the world to be populated by mostly intrinsically good creatures, with periodic spasms of evil, or as populated by stonehearted evil, with periodic glimmers of hope and light, this, too, will come out in your themes. These things, however, are not trite aphorisms found in a dictionary of woodsy wisdom, but are instead insights that only you can convey exactly as you believe them. The beliefs held by the author are important to theme; to put forth empty themes in which one doesn't truly believe is to lie to the readership and do art a disservice. Theme is, therefore, ultimately revealing in ways that might make some uncomfortable, if they tend towards personal reticence.

In order to write fiction that speaks on meaningful themes, then, you must learn the art of insight and exploration of life's lessons, and you must learn to polish your work in a way that allows you to convey these insights to others in ways that do not stick in their craw.

In my own fiction, certain themes recur often enough that one could probably categorize my published shorts under thematic-sounding headings such as *Loyalty* and *Emancipation*. Are such categorizations *themes*? Perhaps.

In "When a Stranger Wandered In," a World War Two veteran makes an attempt to return to the slow-paced American way of life, well aware (after, one assumes, much soul searching that occurs outside of the scope of the narrative of the story itself) that what he has seen during his time in France has changed him beyond recognition of those who knew him before Normandy. The theme of this story, were it to be summarized in one sentence, might be: "In order to return to the life we knew before a monumental personal transformation, we must find a similar setting to the one we once knew, but surround ourselves with strangers who do not remember who we were before that transformation." This theme, if indeed it is the theme of the story, cannot be squarely summarized in a heading.

In similar way, one might summarize the theme of "In the Shadow of Clay Pigeons" with the sentence: "We can hide our shame and guilt from others, but not from ourselves."

Are such observations about life particularly important? The importance of any particular thematic statement such as the two above is relative to two people: the author and the reader. Obviously the statement is important enough to an author; he wrote a story to encode the theme, after all. Only a particular random reader will know if the thematic statement of a given piece of fiction is important to him. If the theme offers some insight about life, some hope, some new perspective, then that reader will have found some importance in its having been expressed in just that way.

Authors should be aware that different readers reading the same story may come out of it with completely asymmetrical ideas about what the thematic statement of the piece indeed is. This is unavoidable, and rather than a weakness of the form, a great strength of fiction. One possible thematic statement for "In the Shadow of Clay Pigeons" has already been suggested. An equally possible statement might be: "Loyalty to one's friends transcends loyalty to outsiders." Which of the two themes one comes out of the story feeling to one's bones may very well depend on one's own personal standing in the scheme of things. Some readers might even simultaneously intuit *both* themes. Others might come out of the same story smelling something altogether sweeter or more foul. Especially in longer pieces, many themes may be brought to light in the readers' eyes. Life is just too rich to mean only one thing, after all, and capturing life—one of the goals of serious fiction—is bound to also capture life's richness and depth.

How to find themes on which to write? If you put your ear to the ground and listen really hard to life, and do your utmost to hone your craft as an author, the skillful expression of theme in your work should come as a natural byproduct of your efforts.

The most I can do is to wish you well as you listen for the coming train.

(FORGIVING) STYLE

I don't know ... if I shall ever escape being more than 'glib.' My voice very well may *be* glib. I may scratch surfaces, suggesting deeper things, never to dig too deeply—but perhaps this is my age speaking.

—Quinn, in a letter to Fred Candelaria

The late poet Fred Candelaria, who for many years was my fiction mentor, once said of my fiction style that it is *glib*. I thanked him for his frank opinion, and then looked "glib" up in *Webster's* to see if perhaps I'd missed some nuance of the word. I hadn't. *Ouch.*

Okay, so that's *my* fictional style: *glib*. Years later, I wrote him my reaction, which appears as this section's epigram. It turned out that Candelaria was not the only reader who considers my style to be glib. A friend told me this years ago as well, using the word *concise*.

What exactly *is* style? If theme is the sum of all the parts of a piece of fiction, its deeper meaning, then "style" as it's meant here is the sum of all the mechanics and aesthetics of an author's opus. Style is the author's voice speaking through the written word. When we speak of the quintessential Hemingway short story, we are speaking of Hemingway's *style*.

This does not mean that an author has only *one* style. Style can change with age, as hinted at in the epigram above (and as will be discussed more fully in the chapter on maturity and growth). Style can also be intentionally manipulated and explored—it needn't be something to which the author is slave. Style may come out of the entirety of an author's work, not considered by the author himself, but noticed by the reader.

As a concrete example, consider the previous chapter on dialog. Some writers prefer to use only forms of the verb *to say* in their speech tags. By doing so, they are establishing part of their style as authors. Other authors purposely (or habitually) avoid all use of *to say*, and this again is a stylistic marker of that particular author. In a case such as this, of course many authors fall into one or the other style camp.

Why one author says *beautiful* or *mournful* and another says *pulchritudinous* or *lugubrious* is also largely a matter of overall style. Actually, why one author gets away with pulling off a hideous word like *pulchritudinous* or *lugubrious* and forgiven by the reader and another does not is a matter of style; while anyone can find such words in a thesaurus, very few can throw them without breaking windows!

How many authors would you forgive for such transgressions? Consider the following passage from Maugham's *Of Human Bondage*:

> They went down again to the dining-room. The drawn blinds gave a lugubrious aspect. The Vicar sat at the end of the table at which his wife had always sat and poured out the tea with ceremony. Philip could not help feeling that neither of them should have been able to eat anything, but when he saw that his uncle's appetite was unimpaired he fell to with his usual heartiness. They did not speak for a while. Philip set himself to eat an excellent cake with the air of grief which he felt was decent.

From *Of Human Bondage*, Chapter 52

Lugubrious. Of *course* we forgive Maugham for such a word! This is *Maugham* we're reading, after all—not some thesaurus-happy hack!

In much the same way, we forgive Hawthorne for addressing the reader directly in *The Scarlet Letter*:

> Under the appellation of Roger Chillingworth, the reader will remember, was hidden another name, which its former wearer had resolved should never more be spoken. It has been related how, in the crowd that witnessed Hester Prynne's ignominious exposure,

stood a man, elderly, travel-worn, who, just emerging from the perilous wilderness, beheld the woman, in whom he hoped to find embodied the warmth and cheerfulness of home, set up as a type of sin before the people. Her matronly fame was trodden under all men's feet. Infamy was babbling around her in the public market-place.

From *The Scarlet Letter*, Chapter 9

There are some who feel that stylistic fiction interferes with the so-called fictive suspension of disbelief. By tapping on the reader's shoulder (as seen in Hawthorne excerpt above), the stylized writer is said to interfere with this illusion that the story is actually taking place as it is being read. The author yells "Here I am!" and the reader is jarred awake. Not all readers read fiction to be put into a state of suspension of disbelief, however. Some read for the sheer pleasure of analyzing the words, the pattern of the narrative, and the piece as a whole, with the style of that piece being considered *part* of that whole. And of course, what some readers purposely read for, some authors inevitably *write* for. Of course, Hawthorne's "tap on the shoulder" is a narrative device not uncommon in the fiction of the past, rather than such a deconstructive moment, but it's a stylistic tap nonetheless, and a tap the reader is asked to forgive.

And then there are the lengthy expositions that attempt to pass themselves off as dialog (even of the internal variety):

So the little thing grew bigger. He was healthy and normal, ate regularly, slept long hours, and yet the growing little thing was becoming an obsession. WORK PERFORMED. The phrase haunted his brain. He sat opposite Bernard Higginbotham at a heavy Sunday dinner over Higginbotham's Cash Store, and it was all he could do to restrain himself from shouting out:—

"It was work performed! And now you feed me, when then you let me starve, forbade me your house, and damned me because I wouldn't get a job. And the work was already done, all done. And now, when I speak, you check the thought unuttered on your lips and hang on my lips and pay respectful attention to whatever I choose to say. I tell you your party is rotten and filled with grafters, and instead of flying into a rage you hum and haw and admit there is a great deal in what I say. And why? Because I'm famous; because I've a lot of money. Not because I'm Martin Eden, a pretty good fellow and not particularly a fool. I could tell you the moon is made of green cheese and you would subscribe to the notion, at least you would not repudiate it, because I've got dollars, mountains of them. And it was all done long ago; it was work performed, I tell you, when you spat upon me as the dirt under your feet."

From *Martin Eden*, Chapter 44

What was Jack London *thinking* when he had Eden restrain himself from spontaneously *shouting out* such a *speech*? Perhaps he had an axe to grind with a few in literary society, and wished to make a point. *Where* he made that point, however, was in the middle of fictional narrative. He threw in a little personal essay, and—well, let's admit it, because he was Jack London—got away with it. One cannot help but feel, however, that it's a darned good thing Eden showed some restraint and didn't open his mouth and *actually* "shout" that little spontaneous essay. As was pointed out in the chapter on dialog, London did slip and later have Martin spout a speech to Ruth, rather than just imagine it in his head. The urge to have Martin stand on the podium eventually got the better of London. Meaningful words—indeed. More than one author, I am sure, would love an opportunity to say those words in a crowded room (though I doubt many could find enough breath to *shout them*). Some great stylistic extravagance that must be forgiven by the reader? Again—indeed.

If you wish to try to pull off such grandiose stunts of style in your own fiction, feel free to do so. Just be prepared to beg the reader's forgiveness (by implication if not in the middle of the narrative itself), and be prepared to receive no such nod of indulgence unless your last name happens to be Maugham or London.

Part 3: Authors

Writers aren't exactly people...they're a whole lot of people trying to be one person.

—F. Scott Fitzgerald

Hayward had one gift which was very precious. He had a real feeling for literature, and he could impart his own passion with an admirable fluency. He could throw himself into sympathy with a writer and see all that was best in him, and then he could talk about him with understanding. Philip had read a great deal, but he had read without discrimination everything that he happened to come across, and it was very good for him now to meet someone who could guide his taste. He borrowed books from the small lending library which the town possessed and began reading all the wonderful things that Hayward spoke of. He did not read always with enjoyment but invariably with perseverance. He was eager for self-improvement. He felt himself very ignorant and very humble. By the end of August, when Weeks returned from South Germany, Philip was completely under Hayward's influence. Hayward did not like Weeks. He deplored the American's black coat and pepper-and-salt trousers, and spoke with a scornful shrug of his New England conscience. Philip listened complacently to the abuse of a man who had gone out of his way to be kind to him, but when Weeks in his turn made disagreeable remarks about Hayward he lost his temper.

"Your new friend looks like a poet," said Weeks, with a thin smile on his careworn, bitter mouth.

"He is a poet."

"Did he tell you so? In America we should call him a pretty fair specimen of a waster."

"Well, we're not in America," said Philip frigidly.

"How old is he? Twenty-five? And he does nothing but stay in pensions and write poetry."

"You don't know him," said Philip hotly.

"Oh yes, I do: I've met a hundred and forty-seven of him."

Weeks' eyes twinkled, but Philip, who did not understand American humour, pursed his lips and looked severe. Weeks to

Philip seemed a man of middle age, but he was in point of fact little more than thirty. He had a long, thin body and the scholar's stoop; his head was large and ugly; he had pale scanty hair and an earthy skin; his thin mouth and thin, long nose, and the great protuberance of his frontal bones, gave him an uncouth look. He was cold and precise in his manner, a bloodless man, without passion; but he had a curious vein of frivolity which disconcerted the serious-minded among whom his instincts naturally threw him. He was studying theology in Heidelberg, but the other theological students of his own nationality looked upon him with suspicion. He was very unorthodox, which frightened them; and his freakish humour excited their disapproval.

"How can you have known a hundred and forty-seven of him?" asked Philip seriously.

"I've met him in the Latin Quarter in Paris, and I've met him in pensions in Berlin and Munich. He lives in small hotels in Perugia and Assisi. He stands by the dozen before the Botticellis in Florence, and he sits on all the benches of the Sistine Chapel in Rome. In Italy he drinks a little too much wine, and in Germany he drinks a great deal too much beer. He always admires the right thing whatever the right thing is, and one of these days he's going to write a great work. Think of it, there are a hundred and forty-seven great works reposing in the bosoms of a hundred and forty-seven great men, and the tragic thing is that not one of those hundred and forty-seven great works will ever be written. And yet the world goes on."

Weeks spoke seriously, but his gray eyes twinkled a little at the end of his long speech, and Philip flushed when he saw that the American was making fun of him.

"You do talk rot," he said crossly.

From *Of Human Bondage*, Chapter 41

Living the Life Less Private

The love of retirement has in all ages adhered closely to those minds which have been most enlarged by knowledge, or elevated by genius. Those who enjoyed everything generally supposed to confer happiness have been forced to seek it in the shades of privacy.

—Samuel Johnson

When you write fiction to be read by others, you give up a piece of your privacy. You cannot avoid it, even if you avoid autobiographical writing. You may be able to avoid your readers, but you cannot avoid the fact that you are on every page they read that has your name atop the piece (even if that name is a penname). For, you see, the moment you form a sentence "just right"—*you* have entered that work. Unless you are a plagiarist, nobody else expressed it the way *you* did. Your ego and psyche *are* there, like it or not, and when a reader reads that sentence, he will only be reading it because *you* wrote it.

The moment you are first published, you have entered a life less private than you had before. If you are to write for publication, you must accept this loss of privacy and learn to deal with it, or you may as well print out all your fiction and stuff it in your mattress for no one to read, or, for that matter, you may as well not bother printing it out at all, and simply keep it on your computer hard drive. In the extreme, if you never wish anyone to read your fiction, you very well may as well not bother to write fiction in the first place.

This sacrifice of your privacy ultimately means your learning to deal with criticism, ego, and learning how to temper some of the negative aspects of autobiographicism.

ACCEPTING CRITICISM

Always acknowledge a fault. This will throw those in authority off their guard and give you an opportunity to commit more.

—Mark Twain

Perhaps you feel that, by using a penname or providing no means for your readers to criticize *you* directly by your true name, you will avoid criticism. Not so. Someone *will* read it, and form an opinion of the work, and by extension, of you *as an author*, whatever name you have chosen to hide behind. You may never learn just what that opinion *is*, but it will exist. Writers are not stupid people, and so, they know this, and this knowledge may burn at them.

If, however, you have been honest with yourself, with the reader, and with the craft, you will at the very least have put your best before the reader, so even when someone does not like what you have said, or how you have said it, you will know that you have presented your piece to them to the best of your competence as an artist.

Their criticism of your work, then, should be welcome, or at least tolerably ignorable. Not ignored out of hubris, but ignorable because you know what you were trying to do, even if a particular critic did not see that. Being an honest artist, you know that not everyone will see what you were aiming at. Not because they aren't smart, insightful people (for they are), but because they simply did not see.

Some criticism is pertinent. Learning to know when the critic is right is as important (or more so) than learning what you can safely ignore. Do not ignore good advice from a critic, even when that good advice is offered in the form of an attack on your work. A little humility about your work may carry you a long way to seeing that they may be more mature readers than you are a mature author.

Once you have absorbed what you can in the way of learning from criticism, do not apologize for work already published. It can't be undone. Some future "new light" (see the next chapter) may come to you, and prompt you to revise, but revision is not an apology, it is a mechanism by which you can grow. If you stumbled, and the criticism was founded on some weaknesses in your writing, there is no need to ask forgiveness. Just move on. Authors "move on" by writing their next work, and avoiding past weaknesses (or even better, by strengthening their weak spots).

EGO, ARROGANCE, & BALANCE

Humility is not disgraceful, and carries no loss of true pride.

—Ernest Hemingway, *The Old Man and the Sea*

Some level of self-esteem is necessary for the artist to pull through often lonely periods of complete isolation during a burst of creativity. I stress that one must not let one's ambition blur one's motives for seeking recognition; there is a line between success for art's sake, and success for ego's sake. From time to time, I have crossed that line, reached too high, for no other glory than my personal need to fly from such heights. This is not something of which I am proud, but something to which I admit.

Unlike ambition or an overly strong desire for personal glory, however, arrogance involves feeling of superiority over others. It is difficult to feel superior to others when even my teenage son is better at manipulating digits in his head than I am, and my youngest daughter can do multiplication faster than I can. That puts things into perspective very quickly.

It is difficult to see the horrors around the world as they are piped into my mind by television, radio, and the newspaper, and feel important beyond the twenty-foot zone around me. No amount of prayer, hollering, writing, or jumping up and down from me will stop or would ever stop one drop of rain from falling, or one leaf from falling from a tree. I cannot do much to stop starvation, bring world peace, stop the dropping of bombs on innocents, or free mankind from the ills of pollution as we ravage the planet. In these things I am entirely powerless and insignificant. The universe wisely did not see fit to give me the power over time, space, and the human nature that would have been required for me to change these things.

As an artist, however, I do have power over those things in my fictional worlds, and you, as an artist, do, too. The universe did grant us gifts. Although we cannot stop starvation by mere willpower on a large scale, we can trade our time for others' enlightenment. We can create worlds where characters conquer their demons, where order reigns over disorder, and where human beings move and are moved by life in ways that serve as guideposts for others.

If you are anything at all like me (pity you!), then you have also been given another gift: the gift of hard times. This gift should keep us humble enough through life and art. Hard times come back in our fiction not to haunt us, but to be beaten into submission and conquered once and for all time.

Authors are also granted a mind that, over the years, will be proven to be able to function at constructing word sequences that others find enlightening, soothing, or educating. We may have been given insights into the human condition that, when expressed in our fiction after meditation, lead others to make positive moves in their own lives. We may have been granted patience at times when others needed patience, courage at times when others needed a courageous voice to speak on their behalf, and wisdom when only wisdom would do to get those we care for out of an uncomfortable situation.

Certainly we have our many, many flaws. There have been times we have cowered when we should have roared, *zigged* when we should have *zagged*, fled when we should have fought, and fought when we should have sat down, had a cup of coffee, and worked it out peacefully. But we

129

can work, through our art, to correct not the mistakes that we have made, so much as those things in ourselves that led to those mistakes.

If we are fortunate, we have been granted the gift of friends and family who tolerate these flaws while we work on strengthening our weaknesses. Through our art, we can find (or restore) balance in ourselves and in others.

Perhaps we have been given more of some things, and less of others, but always the balance will tip left or right depending on how we adjust to our strengths and our failings, and usually, it is best that it will sit level, with neither side tipping too much this or that way. It is this balance that keeps ego and arrogance in careful check as we walk the life less private.

AUTOBIOGRAPHICISM

... she quietly walked away: but she couldn't help saying to herself, as she went, "of all the unsatisfactory—" (she repeated this aloud, as it was a great comfort to have such a long word to say) "of all the unsatisfactory people I *ever* met—"

—Lewis Carroll, *Through the Looking-Glass*

You are a character in your own life. As far as you're concerned, you're the *main* character, right? Who knows you better than you know yourself? None other. So, the answer is, yes, of course you have every right to draw from your life as material for your fiction.

Something to consider, however, is how much right you have to the stories and details of the *other* people in your life. You didn't, after all, make it this far *alone*, so, unless your autobiographical passages are going to be long drawn out descriptions of you sitting in an empty room, you are going to have to decide how much liberty to take with other people's right to privacy.

I refer to the desire to write one's own life (and even the people one has met) into one's fiction as *autobiographicism*. Like it or not, it is a form of Narcissism (and autoeroticism), and probably satisfies artistic ego in addition to simply being a good source of material for one's narrative. Yes, it is a tool available to every author of fiction, and like many such tools, it has its appropriate and inappropriate uses.

In the novel *The Succubus Sea*, there is a "cameo appearance" by a late friend, a poet, under his real name. Because I used his real name and did not hide the details of his identity behind the smoke and mirrors of artistic make-up, I first asked his permission to include him in the novel in such a manner.

You will not always have a chance (or a desire) to ask others' permission to include them (or some fantastic variation of them) in your work. All I can suggest is that you go about such fictionalization of your shared past *very* carefully. I am not only speaking of libel law here, though you certainly should be aware of such laws. I am speaking of human decency.

I once advised a writer who wished to "tell all" roughly as follows:

> Write down, in the third person, every nasty thing you can think about yourself. Write with passion and fury, bar no holds, honor no codes of decency. Roast yourself something awful. When you have finished, having spared yourself no insult and no indignity, put the writing away (under lock and key so no one else chances upon your self-revelation) for a month.
>
> After the pause, come back to your hateful self-attack.
>
> Now, imagine that someone else had written all that poison about you, and you came across it in a novel in the form of some character that was clearly a portrayal of you as they saw you.
>
> Even when the words ring true, some things are better left unwritten.

The above exercise is not entirely contrived. When I was nineteen, I made the mistake of reading a page of someone's diary that had been sitting on a coffee table, open to an entry about me. (Odd how the diary was sitting on the table of a friend whose sister "accidentally" had left her diary on the coffee table the very day she knew I'd be visiting her brother.) The entry about me was entirely uncomplimentary. A real eye opener. Some of the adjectives she had used to describe me were, shall we say, quite colorful.

I had been handed an opportunity to learn the real meaning behind Bobbie Burns' closing stanza of "To a Louse":

> O wad some Power the giftie gie us
> To see oursels as ithers see us!
> It wad frae mony a blunder free us,
>   An' foolish notion:
> What airs in dress an' gait would lea'e us,
>   An' ev'n devotion!

Of course, that was a personal diary (not something meant for publication). The lesson learned, however, was not to be forgotten. I was once told by someone with whom I had shared some events in the past that I *had* been discussed in a book. When sent the book, the passages mentioning me were removed, since the author felt awkward having me read those passages. I left it to trust that they were not unkind, and that the author in question was merely being shy about it. Ultimately, I had to let go of the desire to know what the expurgated passages of that book said about me and my past actions, since it was truly outside my control what was said and felt and how that author had interpreted those things. Don't expect that everyone will take that view of themselves if you portray them in a book, however; they won't all accept it so benignly. And unless you have lived the life of a saint, do not assume that how *you* appear in others' fiction (should you ever appear there) will always be flattering. (This goes back to learning to accept criticism.)

If you simply cannot resist the siren call of autobiographicism, consider instead the notion of the *composite character*. Pieces of him, shades of her, words from someone else's mouth—even some of yourself. Such characters can be an adventure and exercise to concoct. Their compositeness can also be a safeguard against the urge to seek vengeance on any particular person through your fiction. If you feel yourself getting angry at the character as you write, throw in a bit of someone you would never consider roasting. The resulting character might actually be a more interesting read for your reader than someone so specifically like someone from your peculiar past.

You may feel, no matter the counsel here, that it is your inalienable right to portray others you have known in your art. Some may find it flattering that they touched your life so much that they found themselves portrayed in your fiction, but not everyone feels this way, *even* if you have done them no unkindness. Some people—and such is *their* right—are fiercely private, even if they have nothing to hide.

You do not *own* the people you have *known*.

They are not *periods* of your life; they are individuals, with a right to some privacy. Yes, they were players on your stage, and you on theirs, but this does not imply ownership. The moment you make someone you have known a character in your book, you will hold incredible power over that character, and it is my belief that you must hold that role with some sense of responsibility, as the chances are that the person you are portraying will have no say in what comes out of his mouth. Is that kind of responsibility something you wish to lord over others' lives? Do not become drunk on the power you hold as an author of fiction in such situations.

If you are not careful, you may one day find yourself dealing, in real life, with a situation not unlike that of Mark, portrayed in the novel *Janus Incubus*:

"I don't know how comfortable I am with all this," Vanessa said. She pointed at the notebooks. "You wrote poetry about me, too. I don't know how much I like the idea of being interpreted." Her eyes glared with the same meanness.

I sat up in the bed. This same woman and I, the night before, had been entwined like two serpents in bed together. We had spent the entire weekend in her apartment, at one another in heat. And now, after having lost my walls to her, after having allowed her into my space like no other had been permitted, she was calling me arrogant because of a poem I wrote....

"I didn't say anything *bad* about you," I finally said. "I only feel good things about you. You make me feel great."

"That's not my point. I'm not your open book. I didn't even know you wrote poetry." She pointed to the book in which my second place poem, the one I had recited to her as if someone else had written it, had been published. "One day, am I going to read a 'Vanessa poem' in the *National Enquirer*? Are you going to interpret me in some way and send it in to the local contest? Am I going to become your 'Vanessa Period,' some character in some book you write?"

From *Janus Incubus*, Chapter 5

Another danger of autobiographicism is that you may reveal something about *yourself* in your fiction that one day you do not care to be read by others (or care to read about yourself). Once this Pandora's Box has been opened, and the piece has been published, how do you take it back? Spoken words, once spoken, are sometimes difficult to forget. Written words, once written and read, even more so.

Remember this: the moment you walk into your own fiction, criticism of your *work* will become attached to criticism of your *person*. This is all part of the life less private. Be aware that if you write yourself into your fiction, even in part, your readers may start to assume that even some of the entirely fictional parts happened. You *cannot* escape this. Some readers will find it difficult to believe that you didn't do X, Y, or Z, if you did, in fact, do

A, B, and C. By dragging yourself into the dream, you are opening yourself and your life to external scrutiny in ways that you will not be able to control, and you must ultimately accept that the right to interpretation, speculation, and assumption, once your piece is published, falls on the reader. You will not be at the reader's side, looking over his shoulder, to politely remind him that only *some* of the events happened, and even those not exactly as described. Moreover, even if readers are able to understand that not everything that happens in your fiction has happened to you, they may come to believe that your quality of character is intrinsically tied to your protagonists. Do not be surprised if you find yourself defending *your* character against attacks launched against your protagonists' mores (or lack thereof)! Mature readers will know that fiction is a dream that has taken external form, but not all readers are mature readers, and their maturity as readers is nowhere in your control. You will have to grow out of a need to control such things, or you will be writing yourself into some form of misery that may haunt you later.

It may seem that I am trying to steer you away from autobiographical fiction. No, I am not. What I am trying to impart here is a certain sense of sobriety should you wish to venture there. The choice as to whether or not you wish to dig into your past and make *your* life a stage, and those *you* knew the players in your fiction ultimately is your own to make.

Maturity & Growth

"Experience is the greatest teacher," the saying goes, and I think it is particularly pertinent with regard to fiction because there usually tends to be more data in prose than poetry. The scene must be set, therefore palpably described, and the characters must be developed by giving them not only an anatomy but also mind and emotions that make us think and feel with them and beyond them so that we achieve our own insights. Our experiences inevitably contribute to the shaping of our work, but note: our experiences may be and often are *imagined* or *imaginative* experiences, what we think and feel about those experiences and how well, how convincingly our technique privileges or limits us in communicating our vision through our work.

—Fred Candelaria

If you don't grow as an artist, you die. Death is, after all, the antithesis of life. As you live more life, you learn new things. As with life, so with writing fiction. Last year, you may not have felt competent to discuss in your fiction some topic that today seems something natural to write about.

Over the years, as your life changes and develops, if you have been writing all along, your fiction will likely be changing and developing as well. It may not be only in the mechanical areas, but in the themes you address, the kinds of character movement you explore, and in the other issues of life you wish to explore through your fiction.

As you grow, your available tools become more numerous. You look back on the past with these new tools, and perhaps are tempted to return to older pieces, putting new light into your older work by turning short stories into full novels, or by revising older stories such that they become (according to your new understanding of life) more powerful than past versions.

Not all change is growth, or, as Hemingway put it, "Never confuse movement with action." Decay is change, but it is not growth. Moreover, not all growth is positive. Even vines and weeds "grow" and surely as artists we'd rather not have our work become covered in vines, to the point of strangulation.

As you change, you may find that your work has lost its previous vitality, that what you write today is too much like what you wrote in the past, and this stagnation may begin to bother you. Even worse, you may find yourself sitting in front of a blank page for days, weeks, months on end, unable to get past blockage.

GROWTH THROUGH SELF-DETERMINATION

Do not go where the path may lead, go instead where there is no path and leave a trail.

—Ralph Waldo Emerson

When I was twenty, my father said he saw me as someone who had always "hoed his own row." My father, too, had always been one to plow his own field, as had my stepfather, the man who mostly raised me during my formative years. Before them were my grandfathers on both sides, both prairie farmers, so it seemed to fit. I come from, and was exposed to, a long line of rugged, determined individualists.

We all shared common traits. We left home young, made our own ways, and made up our own minds about what life is and is not about. Many of their ways carried on in me, in that I am very often skeptical until convinced, willing to believe and disbelieve based upon what I actually experience rather than am told or read about only, and am ready to admit to when I haven't a clue.

My stepfather's influence in this regard is perhaps the strongest, since, as already mentioned, he mostly raised me. Every event of any importance in life was an opportunity for him to exercise his basic philosophy about matters. When something came from an "authority," I was to question that authority. Who was it who was saying whatever it was being said? What did they really know? What were they *really* saying? Even if it was true, did it apply in all cases? "Who is this *they*?" he would ask whenever I used expressions such as "they say that ..." or "they claim that ...." This was often followed by "Believe none of what you hear, very little of what you read, and only some of what you see."

Statements from me such as "I can't" were followed quickly by, "Is it that you *can't*, or that you *don't want to*?" When the answer was "I don't want to," his reply was more often than not "But *why* don't you want to? Do you not want to because you're *lazy*, *tired*, or because it just doesn't interest *you*?" If I followed with "It doesn't interest me," the return might have been "Have you ever done it *before*? How do you *know* it doesn't interest you?" In other words, Ronald was not one for haphazard actions, half-thought out opinions, or towing the party line.

And Ronald was not just a preacher without a church when it came to his philosophy. Although a logger, he'd read much philosophy, more than he would let on. He could recite poems and lines from Shakespeare, none of the books which found themselves in our home.

The lines of "Invictus" were often to be heard, as were these particular lines from the Bard:

Tomorrow, and tomorrow, and tomorrow
creeps in this petty pace from day to day,
to the last syllable of recorded time,
and all our yesterdays have lighted fools
the way to dusty death. Out, out brief candle!
Life's but a walking shadow, a
poor player, that struts and frets his
hour upon the stage and then is heard
no more. It is a tale told by an idiot, full of sound and fury,
signifying nothing.

MacBeth (Act V Scene 5)

I know now that much of what Ronald was telling me is that we make our own fate, or as he put it, "There's no such thing as good luck; there's only good judgment." He knew, too, since he'd once passed a five year stretch (before meeting my mom), living off the proceeds of poker at the Logger's Club. He was (and still is) also an avid handicapper, marking his racing forms with codes and systems.

"You've got to have a system," he would say when I was just a very young boy at the track with him and would ask what a particular color of marker meant on the form. "You can't bet on the favorites, or the House will eventually always win. It's always going to favor the House. So, you hold off on the long shots, and your system tells you when to bet them. The trick is to have the discipline when they lose—and they will more often than not—to not waver from the system. Of course, if the system is off, figure that out and fix it. That's why it's about *discipline*, not luck."

Self-determination is like that and is a key factor in artistic growth. Discern what you experience. Question what you know. Ask yourself how you *know* it. Plan for your future. Have courage when you fail. Accept your failures with your head bloodied, but unbowed. Analyze past performance and note it well. Finally, have the discipline and faith to stick to the "system" until you know it needs fixing, and then return to the fixed "system."

Or else what? I sometimes pretend that the Shakespearean allusions that found their way into the strangest circumstances were the "or else" of Ronald's "system" for a self-determined life. If you don't have courage to walk your own path, you may end up producing an opus full of sound and fury, signifying nothing.

GROWTH THROUGH PAIN AND SILENCE

Sometimes it is harder to deprive oneself of a pain than of a pleasure.
—F. Scott Fitzgerald

As discussed already, authors who grow tend to have minds of their own. One doesn't make many friends in this world by having a mind of one's own, but it comes with many opportunities to learn. If one isn't listening to the music everyone else listens to, there is time to get to know what music one really appreciates. If one has the time to sit at a guitar, one can discover if one has a talent for playing guitar or not. By taking time away from what everyone else wants and hopes for, one sometimes can see the flighty bird of circumstance and opportunity flying by when everyone else is looking the other way, doing their best to hop into the blast-furnace and melt into one, massive bead of molten cast iron.

And that is where personal growth happens: in the freeze of silence, rather than the whoosh of the kiln. The noise of everyone else's expectations can cloud a mind up until it refuses to grow. Some artists become doctors because they never allowed a moment of silence to let the fiction, poetry, painting, dance, or music come to them. Instead, they let life push them along a route that, ultimately, will not result in satisfaction.

Personal growth also happens in another place: in the pain. Why do people yell when they stub a toe? Because it hurts, and yelling sometimes takes the hurt away. Have you ever stubbed your toe and *not* screamed? The next time it happens, just before the howl leaves your lips, stop yourself. Do you think you can manage that feat? If you can, listen to yourself really closely, inside, as your foot explodes into a million shards against that misplaced vacuum cleaner. What do you hear? Another kind of roar.

One you'd rather not have to listen to, if your wiring is in working order.

Pain of all sorts works like that. We do our utmost to shut out the private, inner hollering by covering it up with overactive lips and vocal cords. We drink. We think about sex too much. We wonder what's on television. The noise that we create to cover up the inner pain deadens our insides to our own ambitions until we jostle back and forth through life in our unending attempt to avoid *truly* feeling what hurts. We may whine our imagined or diversionary hurt, but on the subject of what *really* aches, we hold our tongue. We fight against boredom by "finding something to do." We bury our hurt by "calling up an old friend." *Anything* to shut it out.

And meanwhile, we atrophy. What might *look* like signs of growth are, in fact, the layers of calcification building up, one over the other, until the joint will not bend. Inside, however, the marrow dies. The bone might look bigger, but in fact is hollow and ready to shatter at any time.

What makes one man an author and the other a computer programmer? What makes another man able to manage to be both? Who we are today is the result of how we choose to negotiate with two major influences on our personal growth: silence and pain. The only way we can ever get taller is to find our silence and listen to the roar of our own pain as our lives work from spit-freezing cold to blast-furnace hot. This is where much art comes from.

If you grow as a person, you grow as an artist. If you grow as an artist, you may also find that you grow as a person. Your fiction cannot only be taken to higher levels by your life, but your life can be taken to higher places by your fiction.

GROWTH THROUGH FAILURE

The world breaks everyone and afterward many are strong in the broken places. But those that will not break it kills. It kills the very good and the very gentle and the very brave impartially. If you are none of these you can be sure it will kill you too but there will be no special hurry.

—Ernest Hemingway

Tell me about something at which you've failed miserably. Well, you can't tell *me*, but you can tell yourself, or your reader (if you want to venture into autobiographicism).

As much as we might wish everything to which we ever set ourselves would succeed, life is full of both small and large failures. I fail at something daily. My first marriage failed irreversibly after almost two decades. Monumental or minuscule, failure is sometimes unavoidable.

How we negotiate failure in our lives can to a large degree determine our growth as artists, and this is a book about serious fiction, which ultimately can only flow *from* artists. Failure, then, is a large part of the stuff from whence comes our art. If we refuse to learn from failure, we may continue to fail at things that would otherwise benefit from our experience to the point of our becoming successful at them. If we continue to fail at the same kinds of things, we are not likely to grow, and may instead reserve ourselves to only those things at which we tend to succeed, which can make our art (and life!) dreadfully stagnant and boring. If we fail to grow, we will ultimately not be capable of producing serious, meaningful fiction. Artists, then, have a particular responsibility to learn from their personal failures. To paraphrase Nietzsche, that which does not kill us makes us better authors.

First, let us dismiss any notion of redefining failure into success. This can lead to inappropriate estimation of one's abilities. If one sets a goal, and does not achieve this goal, whether or not one can earn "partial credits" for getting some part of the way their depends on the goal in question. It might make one feel better to define the inability to reach the entire goal as a partial success by redefinition, but the fact is that some goals are not met at all unless they are achieved completely. Feeling that one has made it part of the way may make for good popular psychology, but it does not get the job done.

As an example of a goal that must be reached one hundred percent to be considered any kind of success, consider fidelity. Is a man who seduces his friend's wife into bed *mostly* true to his friend? Is that wife then *mostly* faithful? In some things, close only counts in horseshoes. One is never *almost* faithful to one's spouse.

How one copes with such failure defines his character. In the story "Paladin," the wronged man, Cyrus Drake, offers his forgiveness. As that same incident is portrayed in *Janus Incubus*, however, does not simply end there. The transgressor, Cohen, is challenged to dig into his soul and uncover the character flaw that led to his infidelity as Drake's friend.

"You are a surface player," Drake said. "You touch the surface of life but do not dig into it. Something about your mouth," Drake said, touching his turpentined fingers to the corner of his friend's mouth. ... "Something isn't quite right. Something is sticking to you. I can see it in your novels." He leaned over the balcony.

"You think?" ... Cohen stepped back a pace, remembering what he and Salomeh had done.

"Don't worry, you dumb bastard," Drake laughed. "I've already forgiven you for what really was my mistake. Hell, I should have known better than to give you a written invitation. I'm not talking about you and Salomeh. I'm not a poet like you are, you charmed son of a bitch. I try to avoid metaphors."

Cohen leaned over the balcony and looked down into the street far below. ... He still did not have words for Drake.

Drake pressed his finger on Cohen's chest, hard, until it felt he would almost pierce the skin, and said, "Something deep and dark and ugly is in there, Benny. Something that makes you go around, not quite being who you are. Something that takes you out of your head ten feet, twelve feet, a mile—whatever it takes to give you the balls to fuck another man's woman after he's given you a place to rest your head. After he's been a friend to you. Something ugly, Benny."

Drake took another deep drag. "I don't know if you are *charmed* or *cursed*. I could hit you square into tomorrow, and it wouldn't do any damned good. Instead, I decided to have this little talk with you. For your own good, you know? I'll fix things with Salomeh. You fix things with yourself, or you will crash."

From *Janus Incubus*, Chapter 51

When failure presents an opportunity to learn, if you turn at the door and do not think about it, you have refused to fail gracefully. If you lie to yourself about the matter and redefine it with self-platitudes as, "Well, at least I made it to the door," you are patting yourself on the back for your cowardice. If you think long and hard about how you might avoid that type of situation in the future, you are learning the art of failure.

An important component of the art of failure is the identification of what truly went wrong. To know what went wrong in the pursuit of a goal, it helps to know what the goal is before attempting to reach it. One sure means of failing is to set unrealistic goals. To know what is and is not a realistic goal, one must know where one has failed in the past, and where one has succeeded. This is where accepting criticism (already briefly discussed in the previous chapter) can be of paramount importance.

Rather than setting goals one knows will always succeed, one can grow by setting goals that sit somewhere in the gray zone between anticipated failure and success, apply strategies that worked on successfully attained goals, and avoid those that brought failure to the missed marks. When this approach brings new success, the gray zone shifts a bit to the right or left, and one begins to grow.

This is not to suggest that I believe that every person, given enough effort, can succeed at any endeavor. The old saying is, "If at first you don't succeed, try and try again." Something more realistic might be: "If at first you don't succeed, determine how important it is to you that you succeed, and try as many times as you are willing to allow yourself before moving on to the next of your life's issues." Sometimes, accepting failure and moving on is the most practical, cost-effective thing one can do. It can hurt to leave behind an unaccomplished goal, an unfinished book, a half-written story, a failed marriage, but to spend too much effort and time on a goal because of perfectionism can lead one down a road that has one missing opportunities for success where it truly *is* possible. If you are honest about past failures, you will have learned something that may help you later tackle new goals.

It may seem defeatist to go into something with a built-in failure case. One should not approach a problem at which one has previously failed thinking, "I am going to fail" but rather, "I will give this so many tries, and will adjust my strategy at each try, take notes, and if I fail ultimately, I will come out of this experience such that I will be better prepared for similar tasks later on." This personal learning contract provides a concrete list of milestones and failure is turned into learning about how to avoid similar failures.

Failure is something in our society to which we rarely wish to admit. In some cases, this reluctance to fail has led to a convoluted culture of revisionism that redefines failure as partial success or leads to task avoidance. The art of failure allows us to accept failure, learn from it, and approach future tasks with realistic goals. Although we would like to succeed at everything to which we put our attention, we cannot always do so, unless we set a low standard for ourselves, and low standards have the side effect of reducing, rather than building, our self-esteem. Setting low standards can also eventually delude us into believing that we are more successful at achieving our goals than we actually are.

Knowing what has caused us to fail in the past and setting learning goals can allow us to redefine the boundaries of our abilities, slowly if must be the case, until we reach a point in our personal and artistic growth that we are constantly trying new things and learning new success strategies. The art of failure asks us to be realistic about ourselves and our abilities, to have some humility, and to never miss an opportunity to learn from our mistakes. Surviving failure requires, above all else, self-honesty.

HONESTY

In the second edition of this book, I did not dare to talk about what artistic honesty actually is, but instead pointed to several long excerpts from Maugham's *Of Human Bondage*. The irony of this is that, by avoiding talking about honesty out of some kind of false modesty about presumptuousness, I was being artistically dishonest. I didn't discuss the matter because, even though I felt it deserved attention, honesty is a touchy subject to discuss without becoming uncomfortably preachy. The passages from Maugham were, indeed, fitting, but not entirely *res ipsa loquitur* in their clarity. In this edition of this book, I shall throw all caution to the wind and dare to discuss the matter a little more deeply, thereby risking becoming a preacher.

The first passage involves the protagonist Philip and the aspiring artist Fanny. As artists sometimes will, Fanny finally decides to expose herself to Philip's estimation of her work.

"I was wondering if you'd come and look at my other work. I've never asked anyone else to look at it. I should like to show it to you."

"It's awfully kind of you. I'd like to see it very much."

[...]

"If you'll stand over there I'll put them on the chair so that you can see them better."

She showed him twenty small canvases, about eighteen by twelve. She placed them on the chair, one after the other, watching his face; he nodded as he looked at each one.

"You do like them, don't you?" she said anxiously, after a bit.

146

"I just want to look at them all first," he answered. "I'll talk afterwards."

He was collecting himself. He was panic-stricken. He did not know what to say. It was not only that they were ill-drawn, or that the colour was put on amateurishly by someone who had no eye for it; but there was no attempt at getting the values, and the perspective was grotesque. It looked like the work of a child of five, but a child would have had some naiveté and might at least have made an attempt to put down what he saw; but here was the work of a vulgar mind chock full of recollections of vulgar pictures. Philip remembered that she had talked enthusiastically about Monet and the Impressionists, but here were only the worst traditions of the Royal Academy.

"There," she said at last, "that's the lot."

Philip was no more truthful than anybody else, but he had a great difficulty in telling a thundering, deliberate lie, and he blushed furiously when he answered:

"I think they're most awfully good."

A faint colour came into her unhealthy cheeks, and she smiled a little.

"You needn't say so if you don't think so, you know. I want the truth."

"But I do think so."

"Haven't you got any criticism to offer? There must be some you don't like as well as others."

Philip looked round helplessly. He saw a landscape, the typical picturesque 'bit' of the amateur, an old bridge, a creeper-clad cottage, and a leafy bank.

"Of course I don't pretend to know anything about it," he said. "But I wasn't quite sure about the values of that."

She flushed darkly and taking up the picture quickly turned its back to him.

"I don't know why you should have chosen that one to sneer at. It's the best thing I've ever done. I'm sure my values are all right. That's a thing you can't teach anyone, you either understand values or you don't."

"I think they're all most awfully good," repeated Philip.

She looked at them with an air of self-satisfaction.

"I don't think they're anything to be ashamed of."

From *Of Human Bondage*, Chapter 46

147

The dishonesty I wish to point out is not so much Philip's tactful dodging of the issue of what he actually thinks of her work, but rather, Fanny's view of her own work. She *asks* for his opinion on her work, and then, when he tells his "thundering, deliberate lie" and says they're "most awfully good," she prods for criticism. His criticism is so utterly blunted by tact that it is hardly any criticism at all, but even so, Fanny gets her back up and insists the one piece he elected to critique is the best she's ever done. In short, Fanny is lying to herself about her own ability as an artist.

It isn't until four chapters pass that Maugham examines the full meaning of Fanny's inability to recognize her own mediocrity, and the issues this raises in Philip's mind about himself:

> What troubled him most was the uselessness of Fanny's effort. No one could have worked harder than she, nor with more sincerity; she believed in herself with all her heart; but it was plain that self-confidence meant very little....

From *Of Human Bondage*, Chapter 50

Unlike Fanny, Philip possesses a certain self-awareness that allows him to look at his own artistic path and dissect it:

> The unhappiness of Philip's life at school had called up in him the power of self-analysis; and this vice, as subtle as drug-taking, had taken possession of him so that he had now a peculiar keenness in the dissection of his feelings. He could not help seeing that art affected him differently from others. A fine picture gave Lawson an immediate thrill. His appreciation was instinctive. Even Flanagan felt certain things which Philip was obliged to think out. His own appreciation was intellectual. He could not help thinking that if he had in him the artistic temperament (he hated the phrase, but could discover no other) he would feel beauty in the emotional, unreasoning way in which they did. He began to wonder whether he had anything more than a superficial cleverness of the hand which enabled him to copy objects with accuracy. That was nothing. He had learned to despise technical dexterity. The important thing was to feel in terms of paint. Lawson painted in a certain way because it

was his nature to, and through the imitativeness of a student sensitive to every influence, there pierced individuality. Philip looked at his own portrait of Ruth Chalice, and now that three months had passed he realised that it was no more than a servile copy of Lawson. He felt himself barren. He painted with the brain, and he could not help knowing that the only painting worth anything was done with the heart.

From *Of Human Bondage*, Chapter 50

When the artist is able to be honest with himself, at that point does it make sense to ask for the honest estimation of others, as Philip eventually does by approaching Monsieur Foinet, the art master and asking for a truly honest appraisal of his ability:

It seemed to Philip, brooding over these matters, that in the true painters, writers, musicians, there was a power which drove them to such complete absorption in their work as to make it inevitable for them to subordinate life to art. Succumbing to an influence they never realised, they were merely dupes of the instinct that possessed them, and life slipped through their fingers unlived. But he had a feeling that life was to be lived rather than portrayed, and he wanted to search out the various experiences of it and wring from each moment all the emotion that it offered. He made up his mind at length to take a certain step and abide by the result, and, having made up his mind, he determined to take the step at once. Luckily enough the next morning was one of Foinet's days, and he resolved to ask him point-blank whether it was worth his while to go on with the study of art.

[...]

Philip had nothing to say. He walked silently by the master's side. He felt horribly sick. It had never struck him that Foinet would wish to see his things there and then; he meant, so that he might have time to prepare himself, to ask him if he would mind coming at some future date or whether he might bring them to Foinet's studio. He was trembling with anxiety. In his heart he hoped that Foinet would look at his picture, and that rare smile would come into his face, and he would shake Philip's hand and say: "Pas mal. Go on, my lad. You have talent, real talent." Philip's heart swelled at the thought. It was such a relief, such a joy! Now he could go on with courage; and what did hardship matter, privation, and disappointment, if he arrived at last? He had worked very hard, it would be too cruel if all that industry were futile. And then with a start he remembered that he had heard Fanny Price say just that. They arrived at the house, and Philip was seized with fear. If he had dared he would have asked Foinet to go away. He did not want to know the truth. They went in and the concierge handed him a letter as they passed. He glanced at the envelope and recognised his uncle's handwriting. Foinet followed him up the stairs. Philip could think of nothing to say; Foinet was mute, and the silence got on his nerves. The professor sat down; and Philip without a word placed before him the picture which the Salon had rejected; Foinet nodded but did not speak; then Philip showed him the two portraits he had made of Ruth Chalice, two or three landscapes which he had painted at Moret, and a number of sketches.

"That's all," he said presently, with a nervous laugh.

Monsieur Foinet rolled himself a cigarette and lit it.

"You have very little private means?" he asked at last.

[...]

Philip quietly put away the various things which he had shown.

"I'm afraid that sounds as if you didn't think I had much chance."

Monsieur Foinet slightly shrugged his shoulders.

"You have a certain manual dexterity. With hard work and perseverance there is no reason why you should not become a careful, not incompetent painter. You would find hundreds who painted worse than you, hundreds who painted as well. I see no talent in anything you have shown me. I see industry and intelligence. You will never be anything but mediocre."

Philip obliged himself to answer quite steadily.

"I'm very grateful to you for having taken so much trouble. I can't thank you enough."

Monsieur Foinet got up and made as if to go, but he changed his mind and, stopping, put his hand on Philip's shoulder.

"But if you were to ask me my advice, I should say: take your courage in both hands and try your luck at something else. It sounds very hard, but let me tell you this: I would give all I have in the world if someone had given me that advice when I was your age and I had taken it."

Philip looked up at him with surprise. The master forced his lips into a smile, but his eyes remained grave and sad.

"It is cruel to discover one's mediocrity only when it is too late. It does not improve the temper."

He gave a little laugh as he said the last words and quickly walked out of the room.

150

From *Of Human Bondage*, Chapter 51

Here, Philip is given a frank appraisal of his talent, and despite some anxiety about hearing the truth, he looks at himself as an artist and understands his own mediocrity.

If you are a serious artist, absorbed in your work to the point where it is inevitable that life has been subordinated to art, there will be times when certain questions about your work will nag at you. A fragment of dialog between two characters in a story might seem a big lie in their flow. Something some character does in one of your stories will have you feeling you have not considered that character's motivation closely enough.

You may find yourself waking up at two in the morning, tortured by that awkward piece of dialog or that unmotivated action. Artistic honesty is about seeing your own work for what it is, and consciously accepting when it is as good as you could make it after a full-faith-and-effort go of it.

Sometimes, a truth about life finds its way into your work, be it in dialog, character movement, or even the theme of the work, and perhaps this truth is something that disturbs you as a person. Strike it out, cover it up, or alter the story so that the truth is again hidden, and what have you done? You've been dishonest.

Is that what the character would have said under those circumstances? Is that where that character would have moved, given that set up? Is that what the story is really saying about the human condition? If it rings true—even if you hate every word of it—and you change the shape of the bell so that the ringing suits your own ears, you will likely destroy the work through lack of artistic integrity.

"New Light"

Some editors are failed writers, but so are most writers.

—T. S. Eliot

If someone else takes your words, mangles them about a bit, and produces (even a larger) work from it without due permission and credit, it's called *plagiarism*. When editors do it (giving you credit, but by then you're likely dead anyway), it's called *conflation*. When you do that to your own work, particularly if you do it with class and grace, it gets to be called: "new light."

The novel *Janus Incubus* is made up (in large part) of previously published shorts. The book you are reading now is an expanded and revised version of *On Writing the Short Story*. The novella *Anders' Contrition* is made up of related short stories in the order I intended them to be read, and assembled as the collection they were intended to be.

There's nothing stopping you from combining related short stories into a longer piece and calling it a novel (or novella), if you can pull it off. You will have to revise accordingly, unless you wrote the stories so they could be read that way from the start. There's also nothing stopping you from turning chapters of a novel into short stories, either, although you likely would want to do this with a novel that hasn't been published yet, and then later put credit for the short story publication in the acknowledgements of the novel.

There is also really nothing technically wrong with greatly revising a previously published short story and putting the revised version in a collection later, rather than the originally published version. The words belong to you, after all. They're your property, to do with as you please.

One great danger of such "new light" that must be considered, however, is that eventually the soup can grow thin. How many versions of such a story are your readers willing to bear? You do, after all, have to eventually grow as an artist, unless you plan on giving up writing fiction.

It might be a good idea, when you are attempted to apply "new light" to a piece, to ask yourself whether you are simply avoiding a bigger issue: blockage or stagnation. Are you revising the piece because you feel you can make it better, or because you're jammed up in the creativity department? Even if you are jammed, and even if your "new light" is really just an attempt to get things flowing again, this is not necessarily a bad thing; it just may be to your benefit as an artist to recognize it for what it really is, before you end up in an inescapable rut.

There aren't even any rules of thumb when it comes to such new light. The most I can say further on the subject is that it's good manners to mention in your acknowledgments that some story or other has been published in another form somewhere else. Publishers, too, deserve a word of credit for having stood behind your earlier attempts, don't you think?

AVOIDING STAGNATION

For a true writer each book should be a new beginning where he tries again for something that is beyond attainment. He should always try for something that has never been done or that others have tried and failed. Then sometimes, with great luck, he will succeed.

—Ernest Hemingway

Conflate your work with enough new light enough times, and you will stagnate both internally and externally, even if you have been writing "new" pieces that, well, read like older pieces. I'm not talking about style here; that may never change. I'm talking about telling the same story, over and over again, with different names, different places, but the same basic ingredients.

Probably the best way to avoid stagnation is to learn to see the warning signs. If something you've written bores the tears out of you, as its author, you may be heading towards stagnation. If one of your readers says something akin to, "Ah, another X story" then what you are likely really being told is that you're starting to flounder.

If you don't like writing something, there is no law that says you must finish it, especially if forcing yourself to finish the piece makes you actually *hate* writing. Put it aside, or throw it in the trash if necessary (more on this shortly). Of course, your discomfort may be coming from something other than the writing *per se*, and it's important to recognize this, too. Perhaps you've started to touch upon topics that disturb you, and you're not used to that.

Am I going to tell you to venture into such places? If you start getting *disturbed* by something you are writing, this may or may not be a good thing. I cannot know which side of the coin you happen to be on. You will have to put some thought and meditation to it. (More on this in the next chapter in a section on going to deeply into the darkness.)

Is it really possible to follow Hemingway's advice about finding something that has "never been done" or that others have failed at? There is nothing new under the sun, but there also has never been an exact duplicate of anything you write, the way you write it, the way you see it, the way you feel it and bring it forth—that is, until *you* do it. Hemingway's advice, then, is not as hard to follow as it may seem.

Read something. If you liked what you read, ask yourself how *you* would have written it. This may bring you to new insights about life, and those insights might find their way into your fiction, and break your stagnation.

Finally, you might want to consider analyzing your own opus as if you were someone else doing the analysis. Take a long, hard, critical look at everything you've had published, and you may be able to identify routes and paths that you've never been brave enough, mature enough, or foolhardy enough in the past to address. Ask yourself if maybe now is the time to follow *those* paths. You have new skills, new insights, and the benefit of experience, and it may be that what was too daunting to take on ten years ago suddenly seems less foreboding, and this may get out onto bigger and better things.

THROWING JUNK IN THE TRASH

Most of us tend to think that the piece just completed or the one in progress is the best thing we've ever done. That's why it's always necessary to remember the "Test of Time." I've known writers who went from desk to mailbox with their latest before the ink was dry. Best let the muse take a nap. Come back to a poem later wearing your critic's hat and skeptically review new work under a magnifying glass if not a microscope—"emotion recollected in tranquility."

—Fred Candelaria

Sometimes, after the period of "emotion recollected in tranquility" spoken of by Candelaria above, you realize that the best thing you can do with a work of fiction that you don't like is chuck it in the trash and forget about it. In today's computerized world of writing, that means deleting the document and emptying the trash bin before you are tempted to resurrect the beast.

I came to this realization when I was about nineteen-years-old and trashed about seven novels, three plays, and hundreds of short stories, never to see them again.* The world is better off for it, believe me. (When I speak of *The Succubus Sea* being my "second" novel, what I really mean is the second one I didn't toss in the trash.)

Face it: some junk is *just* junk, and no amount of lying to yourself about how you should store it away like precious coal that might one day be compressed into a diamond and polished for all the world to glory over is

---

* It turns out that I found one of the "trashed" plays and revised it for publication as *Empty Rooms*. The key here is that I *revised* it.

going to amount to anything more than, well, lying to yourself. If you get back to this level of dreck later, you could return to old habits, or even worse, submit the junk for publication as is out of frustration, and—*egad!*—if you've built up a reputation, it might even get *published.* (Perish the thought.)

As you mature as a writer, you may write less that needs to be thrown away. Every so often, a misshapen beast might crawl out of your efforts in an attempt for junk's return, but, having done it before, you'll be ready to kill such atrocities with merciless vigor when that happens.

Of course, recognizing our own trash requires some artistic honesty.

WRITERS' BLOCK

You can't wait for inspiration. You have to go after it with a club.

—Jack London

There is no such thing as *writers'* block. What there is, however, is Quinn's block, and John's block, and Mary's block, and Jane's block, and … well, you get the idea. The reasons any given writer is not able to sit down and write fiction on any given day, week, month, or year are highly personal.

For me to try to tell you, then, how to get out of the funk of your block would require that I know you rather intimately, and I do not know you even in passing. If you're a good writer, you're not a *typical* writer, and even if you were a *typical* writer, I would still be at a loss to find a cure for *your* particular and peculiar blockage.

I could take the tack of telling you what works for *me,* but that would just bore you to tears, and besides that, sometimes *nothing* works for me. I've had blocked periods that persisted across years. In one case, it took me over a decade to finish a novel to my satisfaction. I might even try to suggest some things you might do while blocked, to make best use of your time, but then I would be playing the part of your parent or spouse. What you do with your off hours is none of my business.

All of that is not very helpful, I realize, and one of the goals of this book is to offer some advice and some encouragement. So, what I *will* settle on is suggesting that you consider, if you're completely blocked, being kind to yourself about it. The platitude usually called for in such situations goes something like "We all have our off days." Sometimes those days become weeks, months and years. Sorry excuses for advice, such platitudes.

Are you still an author of fiction if the last time you wrote anything original was a year ago, two years ago? Yes. Of that I am fairly certain. If you've ever been serious about writing to the point of actually writing short stories, novellas, or novels to completion, you are probably *always* going to be an author. And face it, blockage—even complete blockage—is not leprosy; if you never wrote another piece of fiction in your life, you're not going to lose any valuable body parts.

People grow and change. They even grow out of loving to do things they used to love to do. This is all part of being human, and your blockage may be, rather than a little death, simply a sign of a new life as someone who doesn't *want* to write fiction anymore.

My suggestion is to not rush to self-judgment on such matters. There's no need to declare you've Given It All Up Once and For All Time (as did the protagonist of *Of Human Bondage* with his career as an artist after his discussion with the Master, already cited). Your rebirth as an author may be years away, but you may grow *again*, and get back into it with more maturity as an author than you previously had.

The Great Lies and Dangers of Authorhood

The power of accurate observation is commonly called cynicism by those who have not got it.

—George Bernard Shaw

The final chapter of this book shall deal with the great lies and dangers surrounding authorhood. I am not as concerned with the great lies authors tell one another as I am with the great lies an author can tell himself. As for the dangers, well, what calling worth being a life's ambition does not come with a few dangers? While some of the lies have, to some degree, already been covered in part by the section on Honesty, my goal here is to get the aspiring author to open his eyes and become an unabashedly self-critical cynic.

LIE: "WRITE ONLY TO PLEASE YOURSELF"

One can acquire everything in solitude–except character.

—Marie Henri Beyle

As already discussed in some detail herein, serious fiction is about human beings. Human beings, except those who have lived many years in the solitary confinement room of a prison, are social creatures. In fact, even those in complete solitary confinement rely on others to bring them food, lest they starve.

The author who writes to please only himself is at risk of producing work that does exactly (and *only*) that. While he may produce a diary, he will not have produced art. A diarist is not an author of serious fiction, but at best an

158

author of historical records, and even then, most diaries probably make better personal therapy than they do valuable historical records.

Indeed, what one writes should please the author in some way to have written it, or ultimately it might be better to take up something more satisfying to do with one's spare time. When an author stands in total disregard for the fact that fiction is written to be read by others, however, he commits the sin of writing work that can only be understood and appreciated by a readership of one. The poet Fred Candelaria and I once talked on that subject.

"Though the immediate inspiration for [*Chinese Chamber Music*] was a personal experience, I distilled and distanced autobiography into a tragic love between a Chinese woman and a western man who are sometimes in the 20th Century in Vancouver and at other times in Peking in the Forbidden City in antiquity."

The issue of personal emotion versus universality in expression interested me immensely. My coffee was finished and refills were cheap, but I let Candelaria continue on the subject.

"I did take to heart the often violently negative response of many people to the so-called 'confessional poets' and I felt that there was some justification for that when the confessional voice is so private that it is almost talking to itself."

"Yes, when only the poem understands itself," I [said]....

"Yes. But if the confession that's in the poem is applicable to all of us, then it doesn't matter whether it is very much the confessional 'I' that is speaking or whether we see it as apropos to everyone."

"Yes, when only the poem understands itself," I added....

"Yes. But if the confession that's in the poem is applicable to all of us, then it doesn't matter whether it is very much the confessional 'I' that is speaking or whether we see it as apropos to everyone."

He referred to Wordsworth's autobiographical poem "The Prelude" as an example. "In my opinion, [it] fails as a poem because it does not achieve universality, though it is a valuable historical document."

From "Interview with Fred Candelaria"

When the author passes away, so does the meaning and contribution of such a work. While it might sound Good and True (and Idealistic and Noble) to some to declare that such work will *one day* be appreciated by a select few enlightened souls, it must not be forgotten that the author who writes only to please himself ultimately puts his own estimation of himself so much above everyone else that even that select imaginary future readership is not as likely to be "enlightened" as is to be made up of those who are as self-indulgent as the author himself.

Yes, some authors have gotten away with this Great Lie and the world has come out the better for it. Quirky, self-pleasing pioneers on the vanguard have, at times, opened up entirely new avenues of fictional expression for those who came after. If you want to try to write only for yourself, slapping everyone else in the face for their inability to understand you, however, be aware that those who *have* managed to pull it off are very few, so you will be breathing rarefied air amongst the greats with whom you hope to couch yourself. Keep in mind also that even if you do manage to be graced with the company of those who pulled it off; by definition, they will not want to swap anecdotes with you—they will be too busy admiring their own achievements in the mirror of posterity to even notice that you have joined them with your own. Be prepared to propel yourself forward by patting yourself on the back.

Lie: "I am Misunderstood (because I am Great)"

The man who is anybody and who does anything is surely going to be criticized, vilified, and misunderstood. That is part of the penalty for greatness, and every great man understands it; and understands, too, that it is no proof of greatness. The final proof of greatness lies in being able to endure continuously without resentment.

—Elbert Hubbard

Being misunderstood as an artist is no proof that one is a Great Artist. While it may be true that very few fully appreciate what an artist is trying to achieve, it may also be true that the cause of misunderstanding is based in something entirely more basic, such as incompetence.

For instance, a readership may misunderstand what an author is trying to achieve because the author is an unskilled communicator who has not yet mastered craft or mechanics. Who is to blame for any misunderstanding if an author says X, claims to be saying Y, but really intended to say Z? Cluttered minds distilled through poorly crafted exposition are *bound* to be misunderstood. While misdirection is a perfectly honorable and valid tool available to authors, it is a tool used with intent, such as by means of the unreliable narrator. Misdirection that results from the author's not having a clue where he intends to go with a work is just shoddy craftsmanship.

This Great Lie sometimes results in authors who refuse to revise their work past the first draft, electing instead to inflict onto a readership only their first attempts. Those who do not understand that these roughly hewn chunks of rock are not perfectly polished diamonds simply (if the Poor Misunderstood Genius is to be believed) do not appreciate that greatness has no need to apply polish to its product.

I would suggest, however, that true greatness is never misunderstood for long. Diamonds do not sit out in the

161

open, presented for common inspection, to be passed over by *everyone*. If it were so, then how is it that society has elected *any* Truly Great authors at all? True Greatness is declared and the title bestowed at least once in every generation of artists. Society recognizes the truly great, and in some way "understands" them, at least as much as it is able to understand its very best. Those who are not recognized thusly, then, are probably not so much misunderstood as they are self-misrepresented. Genius defines itself, but the society of readers gets to decide who is and who is not worthy of the title Great Artist.

If you are Great, you will eventually be understood. If you are misunderstood, be honest, go back into your work, and try to make yourself understood. Rather than cut off your ear or give up and curse the Unwashed Masses, figure out why nobody understands you, and correct the flaw in yourself or your work that aggravates the condition.

LIE: "ARTISTS MUST SUFFER"

A thing derided is a thing dead; a laughing man is stronger than a suffering man.

—Gustave Flaubert

Just as being misunderstood is no sign that one is great, starvation is no sign that one is an artist. Hamsun's *Hunger*, London's *Martin Eden*, and Maugham's *Of Human Bondage* have in common that their protagonists come through great deprivation and ultimately escape its jaws.

My own views on deprivation are perhaps best expressed by Maugham:

> Monsieur Foinet rolled himself a cigarette and lit it.
> "You have very little private means?" he asked at last.
> [...]
> Philip quietly put away the various things which he had shown.

"I'm afraid that sounds as if you didn't think I had much chance."

Monsieur Foinet slightly shrugged his shoulders.

"You have a certain manual dexterity. With hard work and perseverance there is no reason why you should not become a careful, not incompetent painter. You would find hundreds who painted worse than you, hundreds who painted as well. I see no talent in anything you have shown me. I see industry and intelligence. You will never be anything but mediocre."

Philip obliged himself to answer quite steadily.

"I'm very grateful to you for having taken so much trouble. I can't thank you enough."

Monsieur Foinet got up and made as if to go, but he changed his mind and, stopping, put his hand on Philip's shoulder.

"But if you were to ask me my advice, I should say: take your courage in both hands and try your luck at something else. It sounds very hard, but let me tell you this: I would give all I have in the world if someone had given me that advice when I was your age and I had taken it."

Philip looked up at him with surprise. The master forced his lips into a smile, but his eyes remained grave and sad.

"It is cruel to discover one's mediocrity only when it is too late. It does not improve the temper."

LIE: "READING TOO MUCH X WILL TAINT MY VOICE"

What makes men of genius, or rather, what they make, is not new ideas, it is that idea—possessing them—that what has been said has still not been said enough.

—Eugène Delacroix

Whenever an author has said to me that he does not wish to read the work of some particular author (or any author at all) because he has read enough and does not wish to be influenced or tainted by others' voices, I cannot help but consider that author to be lazy and perhaps even superstitious.

Ignorance does not make for a fresh, untainted voice; it makes for an unsteady, naïve one. That, through some strange form of osmosis, reading too much Hemingway (or Conrad, or whomever) will taint (or otherwise negatively influence) an author's voice, is a preposterous rationale for being unaware of what has come before. While every reader and every author likely has his own list of Must-Read authors and titles he wishes the whole world would love as much as he does, and it is impossible for every author to read every other Must-Read list, the active avoidance of sitting down once in a while and reading other author's fiction because one wishes to maintain one's own freshness or some such is just silliness.

If an author has a voice, or even the potential for having a voice, reading "too much" of any one other author's work will not destroy that voice. In fact, it very well may, by allowing the author to see how other's have already approached certain issues, make defining his personal voice a simpler task than it would have been from a position of ignorance.

Reading Hemingway, one can say, "I prefer to write this way, rather than that." Never having read (or not having read enough) Hemingway (or whomever), one merely goes by vague notions of what one does and does not like. As parents have said to children at dinner tables for ages now: How can you know you do not like some vegetable until you actually take a bite of it? Never having bitten in to a carrot, or only having tasted *one* carrot, how can you be so sure you prefer potatoes?

Reading "too much" of any one great author will only serve to familiarize yourself with how that author grew (or failed to grow) over his entire career. It will give you a breadth of appreciation and a depth of understanding that you will not get if you never pick up his work. While it may be true that everything has been said, some things have not yet been said *enough*. If you read a sufficient number of such works, by many such authors, you may find yourself in a position to understand what has not yet been said enough, and strive to say *that*.

A variation of this Great Lie is that one must only read The Greats, as if reading The Less-than-Greats will somehow cause a form of brain damage that will spoil or destroy an author's ability to emulate that greatness. Having only limited time, one might, indeed, avoid reading too many questionable works of fiction, in order to make best and most enjoyable use of one's time. Once in a while picking up a passably good (but not necessarily spectacularly so) work of fiction and reading it through from start to finish will not destroy good writing habits, but may indeed serve to reinforce them. Who can see a poorly (or even just passably) executed passage in a piece of fiction and not learn what to avoid? In its awkwardness, in the fact that it jumps out and taps us on the shoulder, screaming at the top of its narrative lungs—"Contrived!"— we benefit as authors. Negative examples sometimes serve as better teachers than positive ones; we can learn to *recognize* greatness by exposure to it, but sometimes we can only learn to *appreciate* greatness by occasional exposure to its antithesis.

DANGER: WRITING TOO SERIOUSLY, TOO SOON

Big words are always punished, and proud men in old age learn to be wise.

—Sophocles

In my teens, I read many books targeted at those wishing to be authors. One in particular angered me because it declared that one ought not start writing novels until one had reached the age of at least thirty-five. I had already written novels by the time I read this and considered the advice utter poppycock.

That is, until I reached the age of thirty-eight and looked back at what I had wrought in the more than twenty years that had passed since I had chosen to ignore that author's advice. In those years, I had married, had three children whom I helped raise to *their* teen years, and left my marriage. With every pain, every joy, every happiness, and every sorrow during those decades came scores of opportunities to better understand the human condition than I possibly could have at the age I had first read (and had chosen to ignore) that author's advice. I was an *observer* of the serious life, but not necessarily a *participant* in it.

The novels that survived through those years had as characters men older than myself who had lived more life than I had at the time I penned them. I could write *of* the pain, joy, happiness, and sorrow of a man of a certain age, but I could not very well write *from* the pain, joy, happiness, or sorrow of such a man, until I had been, at least to some degree, that man. Indeed, *The Succubus Sea*, which has as its protagonist a man in his fifties, was first drafted, in a greatly different form, when I was eighteen. What could I have known about the psyche of such a man as Cyrus Drake, even in my early thirties when it was finally finished to my satisfaction?

My late friend, Fred Candelaria, had this to say about writing from experience:

> Our experiences inevitably contribute to the shaping of our work, but note: our experiences may be and often are *imagined* or *imaginative* experiences, what we think and feel about those experiences and how well, how convincingly our technique privileges or limits us in communicating our vision through our work.

From "Interview with Fred Candelaria"

What should be noted is that Candelaria, while *allowing* for imaginative experiences, states that we are at the mercy of our technique as to whether or not we are privileged or limited in our ability to convey our vision through our work. While a certain amount of technique might be attributed to talent alone, what the author chooses to emphasize or gloss over in his writing comes with the author's understanding of what is important about life, and this perspective comes with experience and quiet reflection upon that experience. If an author is to write *convincingly* on serious matters, he must provide the reader with narrative that is backed up by convincing substance.

So, although I do not go so far as to say that no one should write a novel before turning thirty-five, I have come to understand that what an author elects to address might best be tempered by the wisdom and depth of the passage of years. I do not declare only that one should write only what one "knows" but also that one should write only what one "appreciates." The author who exercises his right to ignore my advice on this matter by writing too seriously, too soon in life, risks producing slick words that lack sufficient zest to carry the seriousness of the attempt. Water and stone can only produce a decent soup in fable; the pleasant seasonings of hindsight, distance, and retrospect are best not discarded in favor of the quick salt-and-pepper of literary ambition.

How is an author to know when the time has come to take on more serious matters in his fiction? While this is a personal matter, best determined by the individual author, perhaps a good time to start considering more serious matters is when the author feels that if he were to continue saying what he has said to date in his fiction would be stale in the retelling. When themes addressed in the past no longer hold interest for an author, it may be because he has grown sufficiently to take on the next stage of life in his fiction.

DANGER: INTO THE DARKNESS TOO DEEPLY

There can be no transforming of darkness into light and of apathy into movement without emotion.

—Carl Jung

Serious authors strive to tell the truth about life and realizes that truth is sometimes attired in darkness. Sometimes, for the author's sake, the darkness that lies in the soul best remains in the soul, never finding expression in writing. Just as it is possible to write too seriously, too soon, it is also possible to write too seriously, ever. To reach into the human psyche and grab one's shadows by the hand, pulling them into the light of day cannot be achieved without emotion, and there exists a very real danger that the author is unprepared for the consequences of the resulting upheaval.

It has happened to me, and to others: to dig so deeply into the inky black void of the soul for a truth that the hand comes out of the void stained and tainted, stinging. If you would not consider swimming across a wide river of your own snot, feces, and vomit, then consider that the darkest parts of you live on the other side of just such a river.

Even if you manage to make it through the torrents of the river, grab the shadows, and pull them back with you to the other side, also do not forget that what you *have* pulled back is some of *your* ugliest self. Write about it, and you risk confronting one of the dangers of autobiographical fiction already mentioned: when the reader rejects what he reads, he is ultimately rejecting a piece of *you*. In this case, however, since what you have presented the reader is a piece of your darkest self, the rejection you confront may come as a damaging blow.

Unfortunately, as you do your utmost to explore your psychic geography, looking for material the fuel your fiction, you may come to realize that you have ventured too deeply into the dark lands after you have caused yourself an unsupportable amount of pain. Adrenalin, liquor, coffee, and cigarettes may power your voyage so far by numbing you to the consequences. When they wear off, however, you may be unprepared for the resulting hangover.

What advice can I offer that might assist you in avoiding wandering too far along such a path? If something feels bad for you, it probably *is* bad for you. If you hide that bad feeling behind a curtain of numbing smoke, it will not, in the end, hurt you any less. Listen to your nerve endings; when they are screaming—"Danger!"—you are likely at risk of being in serious danger. Do what you naturally should do when in danger: seek to be safe. The world does not need another truth to add to its collection if that truth costs you your well-being.

www.ingramcontent.com/pod-product-compliance
Lightning Source LLC
Chambersburg PA
CBHW070354290526
45790CB00004B/1492